DISCO

INSIDE ISSUE 6: ACTS, JOHN, EXODUS, JAMES

1 Find a time when you can read the Bible each day

2 Find a place where you can be quiet and think

4 Ask God to help you understand what you read

3 Grab your Bible and a pencil or pen

5 Read today's Discover page and Bible bit

6 Pray about what you have read and learned

We want to...
- Explain the Bible clearly to you
- Help you enjoy your Bible
- Encourage you to turn to Jesus
- Help Christians follow Jesus

Discover stands for...
- Total commitment to God's Word, the Bible
- Total commitment to getting its message over to you

Team Discover
Martin Cole, Nicole Carter, Rachel Jones, Kirsty McAllister, Alison Mitchell, André Parker, Ben Woodcraft
Discover is published by The Good Book Company, Blenheim House, 1 Blenheim Rd, Epsom, Surrey, KT19 9AP, UK.
Tel: 0333 123 0880; Email: discover@thegoodbook.co.uk UK: thegoodbook.co.uk
North America: thegoodbook.com   Australia: thegoodbook.com.au   NZ: thegoodbook.co.nz

How to use Discover

Here at Discover, we want you at home to get the most out of reading the Bible. It's how God speaks to us today. And He's got loads of top things to say.

We use the New International Version (NIV) of the Bible. You'll find that the NIV and New King James Version are best for doing the puzzles in Discover.

The Bible has 66 different books in it. So if the notes say…

Read Acts 19 v 1

…turn to the contents page of your Bible and look down the list of books to see what page Acts begins on. Turn to that page.

"Acts 19 v 1" means you need to go to chapter 19 of Acts, and then find verse 1 of chapter 19 (the verse numbers are the tiny ones). Then jump in and read it!

Here's some other stuff you might come across…

WEIRD WORDS

Cobtrembule
These boxes explain baffling words or phrases we come across in the Bible.

Think!

This bit usually has a tricky personal question on what you've been reading about.

Action!

Challenges you to put what you've read into action.

Wow!

This section contains a gobsmacking fact that sums up what you've been reading about.

Pray!

Gives you ideas for prayer. Prayer is talking to God. Don't be embarrassed! You can pray in your head if you want to. God still hears you! Even if there isn't a Pray! symbol, it's a good idea to pray about what you've read anyway.

Coming up in Issue 6...

Acts: Spread it!

We jump into the book of Acts to read its nail-biting final chapters.

We'll follow Paul as he travels by boat from Israel to Italy — via Malta! But this is no luxury Mediterranean cruise. There are shipwrecks, snake bites, a plot to murder Paul and an all-or-nothing trial in front of a very important king.

But despite all that, Paul doesn't stop telling people about Jesus — the good news is just too important to keep quiet! Reading Acts will help us carry on talking about Jesus too!

John: The real Jesus

You might have heard before that Jesus said He is "the light of the world" and "the good shepherd" — but did you know He also said that he is "the gate"?!

Sound strange? You can read it for yourself in John's Gospel.

John was one of Jesus' closest friends. In his book about Jesus, John tells us loads of amazing things Jesus did that show that He is God's Son.

But there were many people who didn't like the things that Jesus was saying or doing. Jump into John and find out what happened!

Exodus: God is great

We join the Israelites right after God has set them free from slavery in Egypt — but their adventure in the desert is only just beginning!

Time and time again the Israelites have to trust God to give them what they need: bread to eat, water to drink or a path through a mega-wide sea!

The Israelites are sloooooow learners, so make sure *you* get the message quickly: God is GREAT and there's nothing that He can't do!

James: Fantastic faith

James was Jesus' younger brother — but more importantly, he became a follower of Jesus too (that's got to be one special big brother, right?!).

After Jesus died, rose again and went back to heaven, James became one of the leaders of the early church. He wrote a fantastic letter to Jewish Christians around the world. It's recorded in our Bibles today in a book called... James!

James wants to tell readers how their faith in Jesus should be obvious in everything they do — from how they respond to hard times, to how they spend their money. So there's loads for us to learn from this letter too!

**Can't wait to get started?
Then step right in...**

Acts: Spread it!

**Acts
19 v 1-7**

Let's get stuck into the book of Acts. People like Paul have been travelling around telling people about Jesus, and loads of them are becoming Christians! But now there's a problem.

But first, imagine this...

Mel is all alone in the desert. She's had no water for 2 days.

Suddenly, she sees a lake in the distance and runs as fast as she can towards it. She dives in and...

...gets a mouthful of sand. Ugh!

The lake was just a mirage. It **looked** like water, but it wasn't water at all.

Read Acts 19 v 1-4

These people looked like Christians, but didn't follow Jesus Christ at all.

What was missing?

1. Belief in J__ __ __ __ (v4)

**2. Receiving the H__ __ __
   S__ __ __ __ __ (v2)**

Here's what some of those tricky phrases mean.

Holy Spirit

The Holy Spirit is God. When Jesus went back to heaven, He gave His Spirit to live in the lives of all believers. This Holy Spirit helps Christians to live for God.

John's baptism

John told people they needed to stop disobeying God. He told them that Jesus was coming to save them. But these people didn't know that Jesus had died to rescue them.

Repentance

Turning away from all the wrong stuff we do, and living for God instead.

They wanted to please God, but they weren't following Jesus.

Once Paul told them all about Jesus, they were quick to put that right!

Read verses 5-7

Spoke in tongues
God made them able to speak different languages.

Prophesied
Told the people God's message to them.

When they put their trust in Jesus, they (like all Christians) received the **Holy Spirit** to help them become more like Jesus. In this case, there were special signs (v6) to prove it.

Wow!

We can't please God by ourselves. We need Jesus to save us from our sinful ways. And the Holy Spirit to help us serve God. If you're a Christian, you have both of these things! Say thank you!

Keep talking

Acts
19 v 8-10

A	•—
B	—•••
D	—••
E	•
F	••—•
H	••••
I	••
L	•—••
M	—
N	—•
O	———
R	•—•
S	•••
T	—
U	••—
V	•••—
W	•——
Y	—•——

All of today's answers are in morse code.

Read Acts 19 v 8-10

How long did Paul spend preaching in the synagogue? (v8)

— — — — —
— / •••• / •—• / • / •

— — — — — —
— / — / —• / — / •••• / •••

How did some of the people react? (v9)

— — — — — — —
•—• / • / ••—• / ••— / ••• / • /—••

to

— — — — — — —
—••• / • / •—•• / •• / • / •••—/ •

How long did Paul stay in Ephesus? (v10)

— — —
— / •— / —

— — — — —
—•— / • / •— / •—• / •••

Some people have heard the truth about Jesus so many times they become hardened against it.

Not again! He's always jabbering about Jesus. I wish he'd just zip it!

WEIRD WORDS

Obstinate
Hardened, not persuaded by any argument

Maligned
Said bad, misleading things

The Way
Another name for Christianity

I'd stop going to church if my parents didn't make me go.

But look at verse 10. Even though many people rejected the truth about Jesus...

— — — — — — — —
• / •••— / • / •—• / —•— / — / —• / —•• / •

in the area of

— — — —
•— / ••• / •• / •— **heard it!**

Think!

Has everyone YOU know heard about Jesus?

What will you do about it?

Pray!

Ask God to reach everyone you know with the good news about Jesus. Ask Him to help you tell your friends and family about Jesus.

Power point

**Acts
19 v 11-22**

Today we're looking at Jesus' power in our lives.

Are you a powerhouse for God or are you suffering a power failure?

WEIRD WORDS

Invoke
Call on for help

Sorcery
Evil magic

Fifty thousand drachmas
Loads of money! One drachma was a day's pay, so imagine 50,000!

Read Acts 19 v 11-16

These seven guys tried to use Jesus' power to beat the devil but they hadn't turned to Jesus, so they had no power. They couldn't call on Him for help. It's like trying to use a kettle with nowhere to plug it in! They were doing what they'd seen others do, but there was no power.

Wow!

Christians have the Holy Spirit with them, helping them live for God. It's not about saying the right words. It's about letting God work in your life.

The story spread like wildfire. And it changed people's lives in three ways.

Read verses 17-22

1. Praising Jesus (v17)

The people realised that only Jesus had control over evil spirits, so they praised Him.

You've read all about how powerful Jesus is. Do you thank and praise Jesus for being so powerful?

2. Confessing sin (v18)

They realised they'd been doing wrong and had disobeyed Jesus.

When you do wrong, do you own up and say sorry to God?

3. Drastic action (v19)

They got rid of stuff connected with their wrong ways. This showed they really had turned away from their sin. When someone becomes a Christian, it means making changes. Turning away from your old sinful ways.

Action!

What things in your room go against the lifestyle Jesus calls His followers to live?

What do you need to stop doing, reading, or listening to?

Write it down on spare paper and then stop doing it!

Pray!

1. Thank Jesus for being far more powerful than the devil!
2. Say sorry to Him for the times you've let Him down.
3. Ask God to help you get rid of stuff that causes you to sin.

And make sure you do it!

Riot and wrong

CITY CLERK

WEIRD WORDS

The Way
Christianity

Silversmith
Someone who makes things using silver

Shrines
Things used in worshipping false gods

Discredited
Thought badly of

In unison
All together

Clerk
Secretary (an important man in the city)

Blasphemed
Said bad things about

Proconsuls
Judges

Read Acts 19 v 23-34

These men hated Paul and his friends! Many people were turning to Jesus. This worried Demetrius and the craftsmen, as they thought people would stop buying their statues of false gods (like Artemis). They would lose money.

Demetrius knew that when people became Christians, it meant **change**.

Think!

What changes did you write down yesterday? How will they affect other people? Have you done any of them yet?

Read verses 35-41

God used the city clerk to stop the riot and rescue the Christians Gaius and Aristarchus. The city clerk was probably a friend of the rioters, but that didn't stop God using him to help God's people.

Wow!

God can use the most unlikely people to carry out His plans. We sometimes think that God can't possibly change situations. But there are no obstacles He can't overcome!

Action!

Write down the names of people you would like to get to know Jesus and become Christians.

_____

_____

_____

_____

_____

_____

Pray!

God can use ANYONE to serve Him, whatever they are like! Ask Him to save these people from their sins, so they start living God's way, serving Him with their lives.

Deadly snooze

Acts
20 v 1-12

Today we'll read about someone who had the same problem. But first, Paul has some more travelling to do.

Read Acts 20 v 1-6

Some tricky names there!
What's your fave one?

Time to meet snoozing Eutychus.

Ever been in church and the preacher seems to be going on for hours?

You feel yourself dropping off.

Suddenly you wake up and hope no one noticed!

Read verses 7-9

What a nightmare! He dozed off to sleep and fell out of the window to his death! But God had other plans for Eutychus...

Read verses 10-12

Jesus' power working through Paul brought Eutychus back to life. How amazing is that??!

Wow!

No one knows when they are going to die. There's only one way to be ready. To trust in Jesus' death to put us right with God.

Christians don't know when their death will come. But they do know that it won't separate them from Jesus, who died in their place and has complete power over life and death.

WEIRD WORDS

Festival of Unleavened Bread

A week-long feast celebrating what God had done for His people

Break bread

When Christians eat bread to remember Jesus died for them

Fill in the vowels to complete what Paul said in **Romans 6 v 23**.

Th__ w__g__s __f s__n
__s d__ __th, b__t th__
     g__ft __f G__d
  __s __t__rn__l l__f__
  __n Chr__st J__s__s
        __ __r L__rd

We don't know why God chose to bring Eutychus back to life, or what Eutychus did afterwards. But if you're a Christian, God has given life to you too.

Think & pray!

How are you going to use that life for God? If you mean it, spend time right now asking God to use the rest of your life on earth to please Him.

6

Acts
20 v 13-21

Paul and his friends are on the move again, telling everyone they meet about Jesus.

WEIRD WORDS

Pentecost
Special feast to thank God for the harvest

Elders
Leaders

Humility
Putting other people first

Repentance
Turning away from sin and living more and more for God

Follow the leader

Read Acts 20 v 13-16
following Paul's route on the map.

> **Ryan is a total $$£*@$**!!**

> **Where did you hear that horrible word??**

> **Charlotte says it all the time.**

We all follow other people's examples, and not always the best ones! Paul knew this. And he wanted these church leaders to follow his **good example**.

Read verses 17-21
and fill in the missing letters.

Paul served the Lord with great humil__ty² and with __ears³ (v19).

Do you do what you can to serve God, even when it hurts?

He taught them for hours both p__⁶blicly and in their __ouses⁴ (v20).

Are you willing to give up your time to help other Christians?

He told everyone that their great need was repent__nce¹ (turning away from sin) and __aith⁵ in our __ord⁷ Jesus (v21).

Do you take every opportunity to tell people about Jesus?

Use the letters you filled in earlier to form a word that describes Paul's life.

f __ __ __ __ __ __ __
  1 2 3 4 5 6 7

That means that Paul lived his life for God. He tried to serve God in everything he did.

Pray!

Ask God to help you become more faithful to Him, serving Him in everything you do.

1

Acts
20 v 22-27

First things first

Read Acts 20 v 22-27

Now find the verse that matches each sentence on the right. Copy each sentence and its 3 letters into the correct box.

v22				
v23				
v24				
v26				
v27				

...because I have not hesitated to tell you God's truth	S S T
The Holy Spirit keeps warning me that I'll suffer	E O I
I don't know what will happen to me in Jerusalem	J C F
No one can blame me if they refuse to live God's way	U E S
I don't mind suffering as long as I finish the work Jesus gave me — telling people about Him	S M R

You should have made 3 words reading down the 3 columns. What are they?

Pray!

Does Jesus come first in your life? Ask God to help you to always put Him first in everything you do (and think and say).

Wolfwatch

**Acts
20 v 28-38**

WEIRD WORDS

Savage
Wild and vicious

Distort
Twist the true meaning

Word of his grace
The great truth about God sending Jesus to rescue us

Inheritance
The amazing things God gives Christians

Sanctified
Set apart to serve God

Coveted
Wanted other people's stuff

Grieved
Upset

Read Acts 20 v 28-31

Paul compared the church leaders to shepherds. They had to look after their flocks (people in their churches).

Find two dangers that Paul warns of in v29 and 30.

1. _____

will come among you

2. Men will rise up and

_____

_____

_____

There are still false teachers around. Watch out for them!

Find two tactics for dealing with false teachers (v31).

1. Be on your g_____

2. R_____ God's warnings

Watch out for false teachers. Check anything you're unsure about with the Bible and with other Christians.

Read verse 32

Here's what Paul is saying...

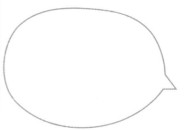

I'm going now, but I'll pray that our great God will look after you. God's Word (the Bible) can make you into what He wants you to be and give you everything you could need!

Read verses 33-38

Work hard for those weaker than you

And don't think you can get out of it!!! *What did Jesus say (v35)?*

What has God given **you**? Time? Money? Abilities? How can you give these things to others?

Action!

On scrap paper, write a list of things you can do for God and His people, especially those worse off than you. Stick it on your wall and make sure you do them! Ask God to help you.

John: The real Jesus

**John
7 v 1-13**

John was one of Jesus' closest friends.

In his book about Jesus, John tells us loads of amazing things Jesus did that show He is God's Son.

Let's jump into John's book...

WEIRD WORDS

Festival of Tabernacles
Jewish feast thanking God for the harvest

Disciples
Followers

Works
Miracles

Testify
Give evidence

In Judea, Jesus was a wanted man! He was fairly safe while He stayed in Galilee, but the Jewish leaders in Judea were out to get Him as soon as He arrived there.

Read John 7 v 1-5

Fill in the missing vowels (aeiou) to show what Jesus' brothers wanted Him to do.

> G__ to J__d__ __
> so that your d__sc__pl__s
> may see the w__rks you do
> (v3). Sh__w y__ __rs__lf
> to the w__rld (v3-4).

They didn't really believe that Jesus was God's Son. And they couldn't understand why He wanted to keep a low profile.

Read verses 6-9

How did Jesus answer them (v6)?

> My t__m__ __s
> n__t y__t h__r__ (v6).

Jesus came to earth to **die** on the cross, to rescue people from their sins. But it wasn't time for His death yet. It wasn't time to walk into the traps of His killers.

Why did so many people hate Jesus (v7)?

> The world h__t__s m__
> b__c__ __s__
> I testify that its ways
> are __v__l.

Wow!

Many people still won't have anything to do with Jesus. They don't like hearing that they do wrong things and need forgiveness from God.

Read verses 10-13

Jesus did sneak to the feast. He heard what people thought about Him. They didn't really know who He was.

Pray!

Pray for friends and family who don't really know who Jesus is, or won't have anything to do with Him. Ask God to open their eyes so they can see who Jesus really is — God's Son.

God's word

Jesus had to sneak into the big feast so none of His enemies could spot Him and kill Him.

Yet Jesus still amazed people with His teaching!

WEIRD WORDS

Circumcision
Boys had skin around the penis cut off as a sign of belonging to God

Patriarchs
Abraham, Isaac and Jacob

Sabbath
Jewish holy day when people rested from work

Read John 7 v 14-18

Who did Jesus say His teaching came from? Go forward two letters to find out (A=C, B=D etc).

The _ _ _ _ _ _
        M L C   U F M

_ _ _ _ _ _ _
Q C L R   K C

Who did Jesus mean?

_ _ _
E M B

How can we be sure that Jesus speaks for God? Verse 17 tells us that if we obey God and live for Him, we'll discover that Jesus' teaching really does come from God.

If we look at how Jesus lived, it's obvious that He wasn't doing it for His own selfish reasons. He was serving God in everything He did and said!

Read verses 19-20

These guys claimed to keep God's law (which He gave to Moses). Yet they broke God's law by hating Jesus and wanting to kill Him. They even claimed Jesus had a demon inside Him!

Read verses 21-24

These people had also been upset when Jesus healed a man on the Sabbath (it's in John 5 v 1-10). *Yet what did Jesus say these people did on the Sabbath?*

_ _ _ _ _ _ _ _ _ _ _
A G P A S K A G Q C B

They thought it was okay to carry out circumcision on a Sabbath day. But they thought it was terrible for Jesus to completely heal someone! Crazy!

Their opinion came from human judgement and not from what God has said in His Word (v24).

Pray!

Ask God to help you to live more for Him, and to learn more and more from Jesus. So that your opinions come from God's Word (the Bible).

Heaven sent

WEIRD WORDS

Authorities
Jewish leaders

Christ/Messiah
The perfect king
promised by God to
rescue His people

Here's another tough one:

*If the Jewish leaders wanted to
kill Jesus, why did they let Him
carry on teaching?*

Read John 7 v 25-27

The crowds couldn't understand
it either. Surely the Jewish leaders
didn't think Jesus was the **Christ**,
who had come to rescue them! The
people thought that Jesus was just a
man, not God's promised **Messiah**.

Think!

Do you think Jesus is just a good man who lived over 2000 years ago and did amazing things?	Or do you see Him as the Christ, the Messiah: the only one who can rescue you from your sins?

Read verses 28-29

Here's what Jesus was saying to the
people…

> **You think you
> know me, but you don't
> know that it's God who
> sent me here. You don't
> know Him at all. I know
> Him, because I come from
> Him. He sent me to you.**

Complete John 3 v 16.

**G_____ loved the
w_____ so much that
He g_____ His only
S_____ so that everyone
who b_____ in
Him shall not die but have
e_____ l_____.**

Wow!

Jesus was sent by God, to rescue
people from their sinful ways!

That was the last straw! The people
were furious at Jesus for saying such
things. Surely nothing would stop
them killing Him now...

Read verse 30

But it wasn't time for Jesus to die
yet, so God didn't let them harm
Jesus. God was in control.

Pray!

Thank God for sending Jesus into
the world for you and me.

Misunderstanding

**John
7 v 31-36**

Jesus claimed that He was sent by God.

Many people didn't believe Jesus and wanted Him dead.

But some people did believe Him.

WEIRD WORDS

Christ/Messiah
The perfect King promised by God to rescue His people

Chief priests and Pharisees
Jewish leaders

Today's missing words can be found in the wordsearch.

P	F	N	R	G	U	A	R	D	S
X	H	C	D	G	P	G	X	K	E
S	P	A	E	C	R	J	T	O	N
L	U	N	R	H	I	E	O	F	T
Y	H	N	C	I	E	V	E	S	B
F	T	O	U	E	S	H	A	K	A
I	G	T	L	F	T	E	B	J	K
N	J	E	S	U	S	Q	E	E	P
D	Q	C	N	L	R	Z	R	S	D

Read John 7 v 31-32

Some people believed that J_____ was the Messiah (or Christ), who had come to rescue them. But the P_____ and c_____ p_____ sent g_____ to arrest Jesus.

But Jesus wouldn't allow them to capture Him until it was time for Him to die.

Read verses 33-34

Jesus said: *"I will soon go away to the one who s_____ me. You will not f_____ me, because where I'm going you c_____ come".*

Jesus knew that He would soon be killed and go to be with His Father God in heaven.

But these people didn't realise that **Jesus is God's Son.** Even though they would soon kill Him, He would go to heaven where they wouldn't be able to follow Him.

That's where Jesus is now. With His Father in heaven.

Read verses 35-36

The people didn't understand Jesus. They thought He was saying that He'd go to live with G_____ people!

Pray!

Thank God that Jesus is now ruling with Him in heaven. And thank Him that you can understand Jesus' amazing teaching in the Bible.

Thirst aid

13

**John
7 v 37-39**

Jesus is at a big feast.

On the last day, loads of water is poured out, and people pray for God to send rain so their crops will grow.

But Jesus has something even better to offer...

Read John 7 v 37

If anyone is t_____, they should come to me and d_____.

Wow!

Jesus isn't talking about a quick sip of Coke when you're thirsty! He's talking about really wanting to live with Him for ever. Thirsting to serve Him. Thirsting for everlasting life.

Think!

Do you really thirst to know Jesus? Do you really want to live for Him?

Read verse 38

So if we turn to Jesus, and ask Him to forgive our sins, what will we get?

R_____
of l_____
w_____

That's what we get if we believe in Jesus, turn away from our wrong ways and start living for Him. But what are these rivers of living water?

Read verse 39

The Spirit

Jesus is talking about the **Holy Spirit**. When Jesus went back to heaven, He gave His Spirit to live in the lives of all believers. The Holy Spirit helps us to **live our lives for God**. What an amazing gift Jesus gives to anyone who follows Him!

Pray!

If you're a Christian, thank God for the amazing gift of His Holy Spirit, who helps you to live for Him.

OR

Want info on how to become a Christian and start living for Jesus? For a free fact sheet email discover@thegoodbook.co.uk or check out www.thegoodbook.co.uk/contact-us to find our UK mailing address.

Face the facts

Everyone has an opinion of who Jesus is.

You've probably heard some of these...

> **He was a great teacher, a good example for us.**

> **Jesus didn't even exist!**

> **He was just a good man.**

> **Jesus is God's Son, the Messiah who died to rescue us from sin.**

WEIRD WORDS

The Prophet
Deuteronomy 18 v 15 talks about a prophet who would come and tell God's people what God wanted to say to them

Scripture
Old Testament

David
King David — the one who defeated Goliath and was God's chosen king

Read John 7 v 40-44

Delete the Ys to show what the crowds thought of Jesus.

**THYISYMYANIYSYT
HEYPRYOPYHET**

_____

_____ (v40)

RIGHT! Jesus is the Prophet who Moses talked about 1400 years earlier! You can find it in Deuteronomy 18 v 15.

**YHEYYIYSYTHYE
MYEYSSYIYAYHY**

_____

_____ (v41)

RIGHT! Jesus is the Messiah (aka the Christ). He is the King who God promised would come to rescue His people. Have you let Him rescue YOU from YOUR wrong ways?

**YTHEYMYESYSIYAHYW
YONY'TCOYYMEYFYRY
YOMYGALYYILYYEE**

_____

_____

_____ (v41)

WRONG! These people knew that the Old Testament Scriptures said that the Messiah would come from Bethlehem (Micah 5 v 2) and be from King David's family (Isaiah 9 v 7). They thought that Jesus was from Galilee, so He couldn't be the Messiah. But they'd got their facts wrong. Jesus *was* born in Bethlehem and He *was* from David's family! Jesus is the promised Rescuer!

Action!

People have all sorts of ideas about who Jesus is. Don't take anyone's word for it — check if the Bible agrees. The Bible is God's Word: the truth. It tells us who Jesus really is.

15

**John
7 v 45-52**

The Pharisees and chief priests were out to kill Jesus.

They had sent temple guards to arrest Jesus, but no one could capture Him...

WEIRD WORDS

Condemn
Punish

Prophet
God's messenger. The Pharisees were wrong to say that a prophet wouldn't come from Galilee (v52). Jonah came from Galilee, and so did Jesus!

Speak up!

Read John 7 v 45-46

Use the code at the bottom of the page to find out why the guards didn't arrest Jesus.

The guards were really impressed with what Jesus had to say. They were even prepared to get into trouble, rather than arrest Jesus. The Pharisees couldn't believe their ears...

Read verses 47-49

The Pharisees thought that Jesus was only believed by...

Christians can expect people to say that following Jesus is stupid.

Read verses 50-52

Who stood up to the Pharisees?

He had met Jesus and had been amazed at what Jesus said (John 3 v 1-21). So Nicodemus tried to persuade the Pharisees to obey the law and give Jesus a trial.

Think!

Do people tease you for following Jesus? It's tempting to go along with the crowd instead of standing up for Jesus and the amazing things He said. Will you speak out for Jesus?

Pray!

Ask God to help you to be like Nicodemus and speak out for Jesus.

A	C	D	E	H	I	K	L	M	N	O	P	R	S	T	U	V

Light & wrong

**John
8 v 12-20**

I refuse to believe that the sun is shining!

How stupid is that? If you shut the sun out, of course you can't see it shine!!!

WEIRD WORDS

Testimony
Evidence

Valid
Acceptable

The Father
God

Offerings
Gifts to God

That all sounds ridiculous, but just look at the Pharisees in today's Bible bit...

Read John 8 v 12-13

*Cross out the words **SHINE** and **BLIND** to discover an amazing truth about Jesus.*

**JSHINEESUSIST
BLINDHELIGHSHINET
OFTHEWOBLINDRLD**

_____

_____

_____ (v12)

Wow!

Jesus is saying: *I am the way to God. The only way. Knowing God is all to do with me. Whoever follows me steps out of the darkness of their sinful ways. They walk with me, serving God and enjoying eternal life!*

But the Pharisees shut out the light. They refused to believe that Jesus was from God and that they needed to follow Him.

Read verses 14-20

*Jesus gave two reasons why they (and we!) should believe Him. Cross out **SHINE** and **BLIND**...*

**JESUSISFRSHINEO
MGODSOWBLINDESHO
USHINELDLISTENTOHIM**

_____

_____

_____

**GODTHBLINDEFATHE
SHINERSAYSTHBLINDAT
JESUSISTHSHINEELIGHT**

_____

_____

_____

But the Pharisees didn't really know Jesus or His Father. So they wouldn't listen to them.

Think & pray!

Do you ever try to block out the light (Jesus) from your life? Are you afraid that He will show up all the bad stuff?
Are you ready to step out of the darkness of your wrong ways and follow Jesus?
Spend time talking to God about your answers.

We've missed out v1-11 as they probably weren't originally in John's Gospel.

Lift off!

**John
8 v 21-30**

The religious leaders refused to believe that Jesus was God's Son.

Next, Jesus told them how serious it is to reject Him.

Listen up...

WEIRD WORDS

Sin
Disobeying God. Doing what we want instead of what God wants.

Son of Man
Jesus. As well as being God's Son, He was a human being.

Read John 8 v 21-24

Now read it again.

This is very serious stuff!

What does Jesus say to people who refuse to believe that He is God's Son? Rearrange the word chunks to find out.

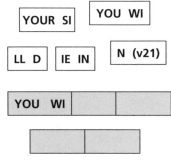

It's upsetting, but true. People who reject Jesus will be punished. If they refuse to to follow Jesus, they won't be rescued from their sins by Him.

So what does that mean?

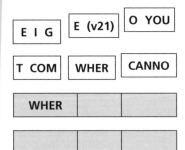

People who reject Jesus will not be rescued from the punishment for sin. So they won't go to live with Jesus for ever.

Read verses 25-29

The Jewish leaders still refuse to believe Jesus. They can't see that He is telling them what **God** is saying (v26)! *So when would people see that Jesus really is God's Son?*

AN (v28)	U HAVE L	WHEN Y
ON OF M	IFTED	UP THE S
WHEN YO		

Wow!

Jesus was "lifted up" to die on the cross, and then was raised back to life by God! So now we can see that Jesus was telling the truth! He is God's Son! He can rescue us from our sinful ways!

Think!

How fantastic is it to know that you'll never die in your sins, but instead, you'll go where Jesus is now!!

Read verse 30: Loads of people did believe Jesus and started to live for Him!

Free for all

Read John 8 v 31-32

What does Jesus say His real followers do (v31)?

Jesus' followers obey Him. And people who obey Jesus will find the truth.

And what will the truth do?

*What does the word **FREEDOM** make you think of? Put an X in one or more boxes...*

Doing whatever you want ☐
No boring rules to keep ☐
No one bossing you about ☐

Yet we could have all of that and still not be free! Jesus tells us what real freedom is…

Read verses 33-36

Who needs to be set free (v34)?

That means we all need to be set free from sin's control over our lives. We're not really free while sin is in charge of us.

Who can set us free (v36)?

Think & pray!

Do you really want to be free? Only Jesus can give us real freedom. Only He can beat sin for us. Anything you want to say to Jesus?

WEIRD WORDS

Disciples
Followers, people who learn from Jesus

A
B
C
D
E
F
G
H
I
J
M
N
O
R
S
T
U
W
Y

Like Father, like Son

**John
8 v 37-47**

Ooh, you're just like your dad!

Are you fed up with hearing embarrassing stuff like that?

However, there are some people we'd love to be like.

WEIRD WORDS

Illegitimate
Having parents who aren't married

Native language
His natural way of speaking. Lies.

Who would you most want to be like?

```

```

The Jewish leaders had their heroes too. But Jesus had some shocks in store for them.

Read John 8 v 37-40

> They were very proud of being from Abraham's family...

> ... but were they like Abraham?
> YES/NO _____

> If they were godly like Abraham, then they would follow Jesus. Instead, they wanted to murder Him!

Read verses 41-42

> They were very proud of being God's special people...

> ... but were their actions like God's?
> YES/NO _____

> If they were like God, then they would love Jesus because He was sent by God!

So who was their real father?

Read verses 43-47

> They would never believe they were like the devil...

> ...but were they like the devil?
> YES/NO _____

THE DEVIL'S CHILDREN...	GOD'S CHILDREN...
Hate Jesus (v37)	Love Jesus (v42)
Don't listen to Jesus (v43)	Listen to Jesus and obey Him (v47)
Tell lies (v44)	

Which are you most like???

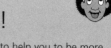

Pray!

Ask God to help you to be more and more like Him, and less and less like the devil!

Jibes at Jesus

John
8 v 48-53

Yesterday we saw Jesus tell the Jewish leaders that they were not God's children.

He said they were the devil's children!

WEIRD WORDS

Samaritan
From Samaria. The Jews hated Samaritans — it was a big insult!

Honour
Give the respect He deserves

Glory
The praise and honour He deserves

How do you think they replied?

_____

_____

_____

Read John 8 v 48

What two ridiculous claims did they make about Jesus? Fill in the missing vowels (aeiou).

1. You're a S__m__r__t__n!

The Jews hated Samaritans, so they were saying: "We hate you!" Jesus wasn't even from Samaria!

2. You are p__ss__ss__d

by a d__m__n!

They were now claiming that Jesus was controlled by an evil demon. Nonsense!

Read verses 49-50

How did Jesus answer them?

1. I h__n__ __r my F__th__r

If Jesus was possessed by a demon, He wouldn't be serving God and giving Him the glory!

2. God is the J__dg__

Only God can judge whether or not Jesus is serving Him.

Think!

How can you serve God more at home and school, to make sure He gets the glory?

_____

_____

_____

_____

Read verse 51-53

Whoever obeys me, will

never see d__ __th

Jesus isn't saying that Christians will never die, but that He has rescued them from the punishment of eternal death in hell! They'll go to live with Jesus for ever!

Pray!

If you're a follower of Jesus, thank Him that you don't need to fear death and hell because He has rescued you!

Glory story

**John
8 v 53-59**

The Jewish leaders were talking face to face with Jesus, and they couldn't see that He was God's Son!

He said such amazing, powerful things, but all they could do was insult Him!

WEIRD WORDS

Glorify
Raise Him up as being great and deserving praise

Rejoiced
Was hugely happy!

Read John 8 v 53-55

> Who do you think you are, Jesus?

> I don't give myself praise. It's God the Father who glorifies me. You claim that He's your God, but you don't even know Him!

These people refused to believe in Jesus. But there was someone who lived over 2000 years before Jesus who believed in Him.

Any ideas who it was?

Read verse 56

> God promised that he would give Abraham many descendants, and they would be a blessing to all nations (see Genesis 12 v 1-3). Abraham trusted God's promise.

> Jesus was from Abraham's family. He made it possible for people of all nations to have their sins forgiven! God's promise to Abraham came true in Jesus!

But the Jewish leaders misunderstood Jesus again...

Read verses 57-59

Rearrange the words to show what Jesus said next.

I born Abraham
was before am

_____

_____ (v58)

"**I AM**" was the name God called Himself when speaking with Moses and the Israelites. So Jesus was claiming to be God!

So the Jewish leaders...
worshipped Him?

wanted to hear more?

rejected Him?

tried to kill Him?

believed Him?

Put an X next to the ones true for the Jewish leaders. Think carefully, then circle the ones that are true for you. Talk to God about your answers.

Exodus: God is great!

Exodus
13 v 1-10

WEIRD WORDS

Consecrate
Set aside for God

Commemorate
Celebrate

Yeast
Used in baking to
make bread rise

Month of Aviv
First month of the
year

**Canaanites,
Hittites,
Amorites,
Hivites,
Jebusites**
People living in the
land God would give
the Israelites

Unleavened
Without yeast

Ordinance
Law

Exodus — Story so far

God's people, the Israelites, were
slaves in Egypt. God sent Moses
to ask the King of Egypt (Pharaoh)
to let the Israelites go. Pharaoh
refused, so God sent ten terrible
plagues on the Egyptians. Eventually,
Pharaoh let God's people go. God
rescued the Israelites from Egypt!

Read Exodus 13 v 1-10

Every firstborn male was dedicated
to God — more about that
tomorrow. God also commanded
His people to celebrate the day He
rescued them from Egypt.

Now have a go at the crossword.

**1. The festival was to be
celebrated every y_ _ _
(v10)**

**2. To remember God saving
them from s_ _ _ _ _ _
in Egypt (v3)**

**3. The festival lasted
s_ _ _ _ days (v6)**

**4. The unleavened bread
reminded them of the day
they left in such a hurry that
the d_ _ _ _ didn't have
time to rise (Exodus 12
v 33-34)**

**5. God was keeping the
promise He made to
A_ _ _ _ _ _
(Genesis 17 v 8-9)**

If a boy asked his dad why they
were eating this special bread, his
dad could explain all about God
rescuing the Israelites (v8).

It also helped them to remember
God's laws and obey them.

Pray!

If you're a Christian, God has
rescued you from the punishment
you deserve for disobeying Him.
Thank God for His great rescue.
We have the Bible to remind us of
God's laws — how He wants us
to live. Ask God to help you learn,
remember and obey His words in
the Bible.

Answers: 1. year 2. slavery 3. seven 4. dough 5. Abraham

23

**Exodus
13 v 11-16**

Let's look at
another strange
thing the
Israelites did to
remember God
rescuing them
from Egypt.

WEIRD WORDS

Oath
Serious promise

Livestock
Animals used for
work or food

Redeem
Buy back

Stubbornly
Wouldn't change his
mind

Sacrifice
Give as a gift

Buy buy

Read Exodus 13 v 11-16

Fill in the missing letters in the
father and son's conversation.

> Dad! The cow is
> having her calf. It's her
> first one... and I think
> it's a boy!

> Do you remember
> what we must do if
> it is?

> Aww, we don't have
> to kill it, do we?

> It reminds us that
> God rescued us from
> Egy__t. I was the
> firstborn son in my
> f__mil__. All the
> firstborn Egypti__n
> sons were killed,
> but God saved the
> Israelites, just as He
> had __romised.

> So we should
> sac__if__ce the __alf
> and give it as a gift to
> God.

> You ar__ my
> first__orn son, yo__
> know. __ou __elong
> to God too. I had to
> redeem you so th__t
> we __ould __eep you.

> What does redeem
> mean?

*Grab the missing
letters you filled in
and write them out
below, in the same order.*

> It means to _ _ _ _
>
> _ _ _ _ _ _
>
> to _ _ _ _ _ _ _ _

This all reminded God's people that
He had redeemed and rescued them
from terrible slavery in Egypt.

Wow!

We all belonged to sin; it ruled us.
But Jesus paid the price to buy us
back (redeem us). Jesus died on the
cross so that we can have our sins
forgiven. If we trust Him to rescue
us, then He will redeem us. That's
great news!

Pray!

Thank Jesus for giving His life to
buy people back — taking the
punishment they deserve.

Pillar case

**Exodus
13 v 17-22**

*God has rescued
the Israelites
from Egypt.*

*But they're not
totally safe yet...*

WEIRD WORDS

Pharaoh
King of Egypt

Philistine country
Where the Philistines
and their mighty
army lived

Swear an oath
Make a very serious
promise

Pillar
A huge column of
cloud or fire in the
sky

The Israelites had escaped from
Pharaoh and now ahead of them
was the mighty Philistine army. If
they saw a huge army ahead of
them, they might give up and go
back to Egypt.

So how would they avoid the
Philistines and find their way
through the desert? Who would
guide them???

Read Exodus 13 v 17-22

*Answer the questions to see the
amazing way God led the Israelites
through the desert. Check your
answers by marking out the journey
on the map (from **START** to
FINISH).*

Example: S1E2 = go south 1
square, then east 2 squares (use the
compass, above left).

1. **Did they use the
   shortest route? (v17)**
   YES = S1E2S3W3
   NO = S1E2S1E1
2. **Did they pass through
   Philistine country? (v17)**
   YES = N2S1E3
   NO = S1E2
3. **Did God lead them?
   (v18)**
   YES = S2E1
   NO = S4E3
4. **Did God ever leave
   them? (v21-22)**
   YES = N2N3
   NO = N1E1N1E2

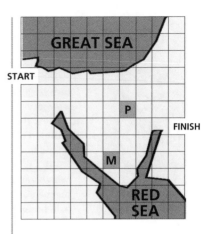

**P = Philistine country
M = Mount Sinai**

God was with His people, guiding
them through this dangerous area.
He guided them by cloud in the day
and fire at night!

Read verse 19 again

Remember Joseph (and his many-
coloured coat)? Before he died, his
sons promised to take his bones to
the new land God would give His
people. Weird!

But Joseph knew that God would
keep His promise to give the
Israelites a great land to live in.

Pray!

Thank God that He guides His
people through life and never
leaves them. And thank God that
He always keeps His promises.

25

The chase is on

**Exodus
14 v 1-9**

*God is leading
the Israelites
through the
desert, using a
pillar of cloud by
day and a pillar
of fire by night!*

Read Exodus 14 v 1-4

and cross out the wrong answers.

The Lord said to Mole/**Moses**:
"Tell the Israelites to go forward/
turn back and camp near the
sea/mountains/river. Pharaoh
will think that you're wandering
around in cardigans/**confusion**,
trapped in the river/mountains/
desert. I will harden Pharaoh's
heart/liver/spleen and he will
pursue you." God said: "I will
gain honour/**glory** for myself
and the Israelites/**Egyptians**/
Eggheads will know that I am
the Lord."

That sounds like a strange plan.
The Israelites were running away
from Egypt, but now God wanted
them to turn around and head back
towards Egypt!

Read verses 5-9

When **Pharaoh**/Fairy heard that
the Israelites had turned around,
he decided to chase after them.
He got loads of donkeys/**chariots**/
helicopters ready to chase them.
The Lord softened/**hardened**
Pharaoh's heart so that he
pursued/rewarded the Israelites.

God hardened Pharaoh's heart so
that he was angry with the Israelites
and wanted to capture them. Why
did God do that? And why did He
send the Israelites back towards
Egypt?

Read verse 4 again

Wow!

God did these things so that He
could lead the Israelites to defeat
the Egyptians.

God would get the glory He
deserved and people would praise
Him.

Pray!

Do YOU give God the praise and
thanks He deserves? Think of
some things you can praise and
thank God for:

_____

_____

_____

26

*The Israelites
were being
chased by
Pharaoh and
the Egyptian
army.*

*Were they
confident that
God would save
them again?*

*And what was
Moses' reaction
to seeing the
huge Egyptian
army?*

WEIRD WORDS
Deliverance
Rescue

Blame game

Read Exodus 14 v 10-12
The Israelites were terrified by the
Egyptian army. *Did they trust God to
protect them?*

YES/NO _____

Think!
When things go wrong, do you start
to doubt God? Do you forget that
He's in control?

For a free booklet on dealing with
doubt, email
discover@thegoodbook.co.uk
or check out
www.thegoodbook.co.uk/contact-us
to find our UK mailing address.

*What else did the Israelites do? Go
backwards one letter to find out
(B=A, C=B, D=C etc).*

C M B N F E

N P T F T

Think again!
When things go wrong, do you
blame other people? Who have
you unfairly blamed and need to
apologise to?

_____

_____

_____

Read verses 13-14
*What great things did Moses say to
encourage the people?*

__ __   __ __ __   __ __
E P   O P U   C F

__ __ __ __ __ __. __ __ __
B G S B J E   U I F

__ __ __ __   __ __ __ __
M P S E   X J M M

__ __ __ __ __
G J H I U

__ __ __   __ __ __.
G P S   Z P V

Moses **trusted God**. He knew that
God would fight for the Israelites.
It wasn't down to them — they
just had to be still (v14). God was
in control and He would rescue His
people again.

Pray!
Say sorry to God for times you've
doubted Him or blamed other
people. Ask Him to help you
TRUST Him more, knowing that
He is in control.

27

**Exodus
14 v 15-20**

The mighty Egyptian army was hot on the heels of the Israelites.

God's people were terrified.

WEIRD WORDS

Staff
Like a walking stick

Horsemen
Soldiers on horses

God is in control

Read Exodus 14 v 15-18

Fill in the missing vowels (aeiou) to answer the questions.

What did God tell Moses to do (v16)?

Str__tch his st__ff out over the s_ _ to d__v__d__ the w__t__r so the __sr__ __l__t__s could go through on dry gr__ __nd

God would guide the Israelites to safety. Why did He do it this way (v18)?

So the __gypt__ __ns will kn__w th__t I am the L__rd

Wow!

God wants people to know that He is in control of everything. To know that He is the only God. He wants people to worship Him.

Read verses 19-20

Have a go at drawing what happened. If that's too tricky, describe it in your own words.

God put the pillar of cloud in between the Israelites and the Egyptians, protecting His people. He also gave the Israelites light and plunged the Egyptians into total darkness.

Wow!

God looks after His people. That doesn't mean that things will be easy for Christians. But they can turn to God for help and He's always with them.

Pray!

Thank God that He wants EVERYONE to know the truth that He is Lord.

No escape!

God has
rescued the
Israelites from
slavery.

But Pharaoh
and the
Egyptians are
giving chase
and appear to
have trapped
the Israelites
next to the
Red Sea.

But God was about to do something incredible...

Read Exodus 14 v 21-31

Just imagine the scene. As morning begins to dawn, the Egyptians can see
the Israelites escaping through the sea. Furious, they charge after them — but
soon slow down. Their chariot wheels
have stuck and some are even falling off!
They realise too late what's happening.

The L_____ is fighting
against us! (v25)

Wow!

They got the punishment they
deserved for going against God.
God punishes everyone who
refuses to obey Him.

Write down **every second letter** on the chariot wheels to find a verse to
remember (Hebrews 10 v 31). Start with the circled (I)

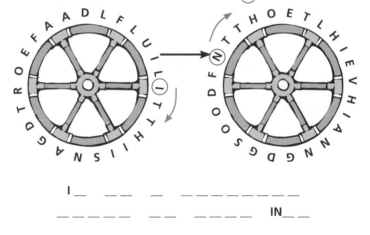

I_ __ _ _ _ _ _ _ _ _

_ _ _ _ _ _ _ _ _ _ _ IN_ _

_ _ _ _ _ _ _ _ _ _ _ _ _

_ _ _ _ _ _ _ _ _

One day, God will punish everyone
who has chosen to live for
themselves and ignore Him. But He
rescues everyone who obeys Him,
just as He rescued the Israelites.

Pray!

Pray for people you know who
need rescuing by God. Ask Him to
change their lives around, so they
start living His way.

19

**Exodus
15 v 1-10**

WEIRD WORDS

Highly exalted
Praised loads

Salvation
Rescue

Right hand
God's power

Majestic
Like a king. In charge.

Opposed you
Were against you

Unleashed
Released

Consumed like stubble
Destroyed like burning crops

The spoils
Things taken from an enemy

Gorge myself
Eat them greedily

Sing when you're winning

At church or in the shower? Where do you sing loudest?

_____

_____

_____

God had rescued the Israelites from the evil Egyptians. He'd miraculously helped them to walk through the Red Sea and then drowned their enemies! Now Moses wants to sing about it!

Read Exodus 15 v 1-10

Moses praised God for rescuing them and destroying their enemies.

Read verse 2 again

… And to see how Moses described God.

The Lord is my strength, my strong defender.

The Israelites had been helpless. But God had easily killed their enemies.

Do you feel helpless? Is God YOUR strength? Only He can defeat your worst enemy – sin.

He is my God, and I will praise Him.

They had nothing to boast about. God was the only one deserving of praise.

Does God's goodness make YOU sing? Does He make you happy? Is He the one you praise?

The Lord is my salvation, the one who saved me.

God rescued them from the Egyptian army.

Has Jesus rescued YOU? He's the only hope we have of being saved from our sinful ways.

Want to know how Jesus can rescue you? For the free e-booklet
What's it all about?
email
discover@thegoodbook.co.uk
or check out
www.thegoodbook.co.uk/contact-us
to find our UK mailing address.

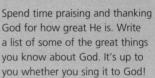

Pray!

Spend time praising and thanking God for how great He is. Write a list of some of the great things you know about God. It's up to you whether you sing it to God!

Raise the praise

**Exodus
15 v 11-21**

WEIRD WORDS

The gods
Fake gods

Majestic in holiness
The perfect King

Working wonders
Doing miracles

Holy dwelling
Special place

Anguish
Fear and worry

Dread
Great fear

Inheritance
The land God will give them

Sanctuary
Holy place

Reigns
Rules as King

Moses was singing to God, thanking and praising Him for rescuing them. Suddenly the future didn't seem so hard for the Israelites to face. There were lots of enemies ahead of them, but no enemy was as powerful as God!

Read Exodus 15 v 11-19

Now fill in the blanks by unscrambling the backwards codes and putting them in the right boxes below.

DAERDDNARORRET

YLEFASMEHTDAEL

MEHTDEWOLLAWSHTRAEEHT

What had happened to God's enemies (v12)?

T_____

_____

What would happen to any other enemies (v16)?
They would be filled with

T_____

_____

What could Israel expect for themselves (v17)?

That God would L_____

_____

into the promised land

Read verses 20-21

Miriam and all the Israelite women joined in singing to God too! Everyone was so happy that God was with them!

Wow!

Christians can be just as confident in God as Moses and Miriam were. God has already done so much for Christians, rescuing them from sin.

They know that no enemy is strong enough to stop them having eternal life. Like the Israelites, they know that God is King over everything!

Pray!

Read verse 18. Praise and thank God that He's so powerful. Nothing can defeat Him. He is King for ever!

Trust and obey

**Exodus
15 v 22-27**

The Israelites had walked through the Red Sea and God had destroyed their enemies, the Egyptians.

The Israelites were in a great mood.

But not for long...

WEIRD WORDS

Decrees
Commands

Springs
Where fresh water springs up from under the ground

Read Exodus 15 v 22-24

How long before they started grumbling?

| _____ days! |

They were in the desert with no clean water to drink, so it's not surprising they grumbled. But they had already forgotten that God had done amazing things for them and He was with them all the way.

Think!

When things go wrong, do you forget about God? Do you spend more time moaning than turning to Him for help?

*Cross out all the **A**s, **B**s and **C**s then write out what's left, to reveal **Psalm 54 v 4**.*

**C A B C G O A C B A C C D
I C B B C C A B C A S C C A B A C
M B C B A C C Y B B H C A B E C
A B L A C C B P A C B A B C B**

G_____

_____

Wow!

God is always with His people, and longs to help them. They can turn to Him and ask Him for help at any time.

As always, God had a very good reason for not giving them fresh water immediately. He was **testing** the Israelites to see if they still **trusted** Him.

Read Exodus 15 v 25-27

God made the water sweet and drinkable. God said that if the people obeyed His laws, then they wouldn't suffer nasty diseases as the Egyptians had. God was showing them how important it is to **obey** Him.

And look at the great place God gave them to rest and drink fresh water!

Pray!

Ask God to help you TRUST Him more and turn to Him when things go wrong. Maybe you need to ask His help with something right now...
And ask God to help you OBEY Him, and do what the Bible says.

Acts: Spread it!

Acts
21 v 1-16

Acts is all about Jesus' followers (like Paul) travelling to tell people the great news of Jesus.

So let's see where Paul and his friends have reached now.

Read Acts 21 v 1-6

Where did they travel? Fill in the destinations and follow the route on the map.

1. K _____

2. R _____

3. P _____

4. P _____

5. C _____

6. T _____

Some Jewish people hated Paul telling Jews about Jesus. They wanted to kill Paul. Jerusalem was the main city for Jewish people.

So what did Paul's friends say to him? (Look at verse 4!)

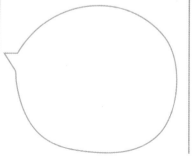

Read verses 7-11

Where did they go next (v7-8)?

7. P _____

8. C _____

Check out what Agabus did (v11). The Holy Spirit was warning Paul that he would be thrown into prison if he went to Jerusalem. Surely Paul would take these hints and stay away from Jerusalem...

Read verses 12-16

Fill in Paul's surprising words from verse 13.

**I am ready to d_____
in J_____
for the name of the
Lord J_____**

Wow! Nothing would stop Paul telling people about Jesus. He was prepared to be thrown in prison or even die for Jesus if he had to!

Think & pray!

We're often terrified of a little teasing! If we love Jesus then we'll be prepared to suffer for talking about Him. Ask God to give you the courage to speak out for Jesus.

33

**Acts
21 v 17-36**

Paul in trouble

Paul's friends warned him not to go to Jerusalem because they knew he would be arrested or even murdered there. But nothing would stop Paul telling the people of Jerusalem about Jesus!

Read Acts 21 v 17-26

Confused about what's going on? Here are the basics...

WEIRD WORDS

Brothers and sisters
Christians

Gentiles
Non-Jews

Zealous
Enthusiastic

Circumcise
Cut off skin around the penis

Vow
Promise to God

Purification rights
Special ceremony

Abstain
Don't do it

Sacrificed to idols
Offered to false gods

Defiled
Made unclean

Jerusalem newsflash

• Paul met with James and other Christian leaders (v18).

• They told Paul that many Jews believed in Jesus dying for their sins! (v20)

• There were false rumours that Paul had told people to stop obeying God's Old Testament laws (v21).

• To prove that he still followed God's laws, Paul helped four men to serve God in a special way (that's what the vow and purifying stuff is all about).

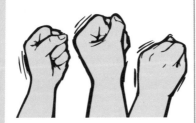

Paul was careful not to offend these Jewish Christians. He wanted to show that he obeyed God just as they did.

Think!

What can you do to get along better with Christians who are different from you?

_____

_____

_____

_____

You don't have to agree on everything! But it's great when Christians find ways to serve God together.

Read verses 27-36

Some of the Jews wanted to see Paul dead. They lied about him so that the crowd attacked Paul, trying to kill him. But Roman soldiers stopped them.

Christians can face angry opposition for telling the truth about Jesus. People often tell lies about Christians to turn others against them.

Pray!

Ask God to help you cope with any opposition you face for being a Christian. And ask Him to help you get on better with other Christians so that you can serve Him together.

What's your story?

**Acts
21 & 22**

WEIRD WORDS

Barracks
Soldiers' base

Revolt
Sold

Aramaic
Jewish language

Gamaliel
Great Jewish teacher

Zealous
Enthusiastic

Persecuted
Attacked

The Way
Christianity

Devout observer
He obeyed God's law

Righteous One
Jesus Christ

Martyr
Person who died for their beliefs

Some of the Jews in Jerusalem turned the crowds against Paul so they attacked and nearly killed him. But Roman soldiers stopped them and arrested Paul.

Read Acts 21 v 37-40

Because Paul was a Roman citizen, the Roman commander allowed Paul to speak to the angry crowd. He had a great story to tell them…

Read Acts 22 v 1-21

Now number the parts of Paul's story in the right order.

○ **Ananias gave me back my sight**

① **I am a Jew and I was trained by Gamaliel, a great Jewish teacher**

○ **Jesus appeared to me and told me to go to Damascus**

○ **On the way to Damascus a bright light from heaven flashed around me**

○ **He told me to leave Jerusalem and go to tell the Gentiles about Him**

○ **I persecuted Christians; arresting some, killing others**

○ **I went into a trance and Jesus appeared to me**

○ **Ananias told me I would tell people about Jesus and that I should be baptised to show that Jesus had washed my sins away**

What an amazing story!

You might not have a story as spectacular as that, but all **Christians** have a story to tell about how Jesus has changed their lives. It may not sound exciting to you, but other people will find your story exciting.

Action!

Grab some spare paper. Take time to write down the story of how Jesus has changed your life. Don't try to make it spectacular — just tell the truth. Then learn it by heart so you can easily tell other people your story.

Pray!

Ask God to give you the courage and opportunities to tell people your story. Ask Him to use your story to introduce people to Jesus so they get to know Him.

Heavenly home

Paul told the angry crowd the story of how Jesus changed his life.

But they still wanted to kill him...

Read Acts 22 v 22-24

Things aren't looking good for Paul. The crowd want him dead and the Roman soldiers are about to tie him to a post and cruelly whip him, tearing the flesh from his back…

Read verses 25-30

Just as they were about to whip him, what did Paul say? Fill in the missing vowels to find out.

> Is it l__gal for you to fl__g a R__m__n c__t__z__n who hasn't even been f__ __nd g__ __lty?

Roman law

According to Roman law, it was illegal to whip or torture a Roman citizen. Paul was a Roman citizen so they couldn't flog him.

Where do you come from?

_____

How do you feel about coming from there? Proud? Embarrassed? Not bothered?

_____

_____

_____

*If you're a Christian, Paul says you're a citizen of a far better place! Find **Philippians 3 v 20-21** in your Bible. Add the vowels to complete Paul's great news.*

Our citizenship is in h__ __v__n. We eagerly await a S__v__o__r from there, the L__rd J__s__s Chr__st, who will tr__nsf__rm our b__d__ __s so that they will be like his gl__ri__ __us b__dy!

Wow!

Christians belong to heaven. Because Jesus has rescued them, one day they will go to live with Him! And they will become more like Jesus! There's loads to thank God for — so start right now!

White lies

The Jewish crowd wanted to kill Paul because he was preaching about Jesus.

Roman soldiers arrested Paul but couldn't torture him because he was a Roman citizen.

WEIRD WORDS

Good conscience
Paul knew that he had obeyed God

High priest
Most important Jewish leader

Violate
Break the law

So they handed Paul over to the Jewish court — the Sanhedrin. What would they do with him?

Read Acts 23 v 1-2
Paul told the Sanhedrin that he was serving God and had done nothing wrong. What did Ananias the high priest command them to do?
Go back one letter to find out.

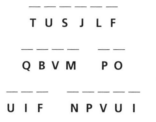

— — — — — —
T U S J L F

— — — — — —
Q B V M   P O

— — — — — — — —
U I F   N P V U I

This was against the Jewish law. They were not allowed to treat Paul like that.

Read verses 3-5
What did Paul call Ananias?

— — — — — — — —
Z P V   X I J U F

— — — — — —
X B T I F E

— — — —
X B M M

Paul was probably calling Ananias a hypocrite: someone who says one thing but does the opposite. Like a building with a bright white outside that is dirty on the inside.

Ananias appeared to be godly but he didn't really obey God.

He accused Paul of breaking God's law yet broke it himself!

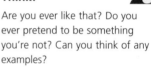

Think!
Are you ever like that? Do you ever pretend to be something you're not? Can you think of any examples?

_____

_____

_____

_____

Pray!

Talk to God about times you've been hypocritical. Say sorry to Him. Ask God to help you live in a way that truly pleases Him, not just pretending to.

Sad, you see?

**Acts
23 v 6-11**

Paul is on trial in the most important Jewish court.

The Jewish leaders want to kill him because he keeps telling people how Jesus can rescue them from their sin.

Before we read today's Bible bit, we need a quick history lesson...

Sadducees

A group of Jews who did not believe in the resurrection of the dead. That means they didn't believe in eternal life. They thought that once you died that was it. They also did not believe in angels or spirits.

Pharisees

A powerful group of Jews who did believe in eternal life and angels and spirits.

Read Acts 3 v 6-10

Paul mentioned that he was brought up as a Pharisee. He also said that he believed in eternal life with God. This caused chaos with the Pharisees and Sadducees arguing violently!

Read verse 11

What did God promise Paul?

> **Just as you have told people about me here in J_____, so you must also do the same in R_____.**

God promised Paul that he wouldn't die in Jerusalem and he would get the chance to tell people about Jesus in Rome. Later, we'll see if God kept His promise.

Wow!

God has a great promise for Christians. Everyone who trusts in Jesus' death in their place will have their sins forgiven. And they will go to live with God forever! Christians have no need to be sad like the Sadducees!

WEIRD WORDS

Vigorously
Aggressively

Testified
Told people about God. Given evidence that Jesus died and was raised back to life.

Pray!

Thank God that, unlike the Sadducees, we have the certain hope of eternal life with Him!

Pharisee

Sadducee

38

Acts
23 v 12-35

Paul's friends have been worried that he would be killed in Jerusalem.

WEIRD WORDS

Conspiracy
Plot to kill Paul

Petition
Ask, put pressure on him

Pretext
Excuse

Consent
Agreement

Detachment
Military group

Cavalry
Soldiers on horses

Saved by the cavalry

An angry crowd had attacked Paul and he was now a prisoner of the Roman soldiers. But God had promised Paul that he would live to go and preach in Rome. What will happen next?

Read Acts 23 v 12-15

and cross out the wrong answers.

A group of over 30/40 Jews made an oath not to eat or drink/smoke until they had tickled/killed Paul. The plan was to persuade the Roman commander/condor to send Paul to the Sanhedrin/sandpit again. They would kill Paul before/after he got there. It's not looking good for Paul!

Read verses 16-22

The son of Paul's auntie/sister/brother overheard the plot. He told the Jewish/Roman commander all about the plant/pot/plot. The commander told him not to tell/smell anyone.

Read verses 23-35

The commander ordered 200 soldiers, 70 birdmen/horsemen and 200 spearmints/spearmen to take Paul to Governor Felix/Whiskers in Caesarea/Syria. He sent a present/letter to Felix explaining the situation. Felix said he would hear Paul's case when his accusers/friends arrived.

God had promised to keep Paul safe in Jerusalem. Even though many people wanted to kill him, Paul still made it safely to Caesarea. Maybe he would get to Rome after all...

Wow!

God always keeps His promises — often in the most amazing ways. Check out one of God's great promises in John 5 v 24. Whoever trusts Jesus to rescue them will live for ever with God! And that's a promise!

Pray!

Thank God that He keeps His word. Thank Him that anyone who trusts Jesus to rescue them will have eternal life with Him.

Opportunity knocks

Acts
24 v 1-27

Paul has been sent to appear before governor Felix for a trial.

The Jewish leaders are hoping he will be sentenced to death. *Today's missing words are in the **backwards** word pool.*

> diarfa   develieb   owt
> eslaf   xileF   tsirhC
> elpmet   yltneuqerf
> devorp   stoir
> suseJ   deppihsrow

Read Acts 24 v 1-9

Ananias the high priest made lots of f_____ accusations against Paul. He said that Paul had started r_____ (v5) and had wrecked the t_____ (v6). All lies.

Read verses 10-21

Paul said that none of these charges against him could be p_____ (v13). He admitted that he w_____ God (v14), was a Christian and b_____ everything written in the Old Testament.

Action!

Paul took this opportunity to share his Christian beliefs. Do you ever mention your beliefs in conversation? Think of how you can slip it into chats this week. Maybe mentioning what you did at church/ youth group.

Read verses 22-27

Governor F_____ treated Paul well (v23). He listened to Paul talk about his faith in C_____ J_____ (v24), explaining what it means to be a Christian. Felix was a_____ of what he heard (v25) but he didn't turn to God. Paul was kept in prison for t_____ years and Felix talked with him f_____ (v26).

Pray!

Ask God to help you talk about Him in your conversations. Ask Him to help you stick at it even when it means many frustrating conversations.

Romeward bound

Acts
25 v 1-27

Paul is still on trial! He's being passed around from court to court but no one can prove that he's done anything wrong.

WEIRD WORDS

Province
State or county

Convened
Brought together

Conferred
Talked stuff over

Condemned
Sentenced to death

Great pomp
Showing magnificence

Petitioned
Pressured

Read Acts 25 v 1-12

The Jewish leaders made another plot to kill Paul (v3) but God didn't allow it to happen.

So the Jews made more false accusations against Paul which they couldn't prove (v7).

Go back one letter to reveal what Paul said.

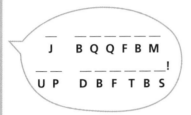

J   B Q Q F B M

__ __   D B F T B S !
U P

Paul wanted to go to Rome so Emperor Caesar would meet him. Then even more people would hear Paul talk about Jesus! Festus agreed to send him to Caesar in Rome.

Why is this so amazing?

Look up Acts 23 v 11.

__ __ __
H P E

__ __ __ __ __ __ __ __
Q S P N J T F E

__ __ __ __   __ __ __ __
U I B U   Q B V M

__ __ __ __ __   __ __
X P V M E   H P

__ __   __ __ __ __
U P   S P N F

Yet again, God was keeping His promises. He always does!

In **Acts 25 v 13-22** we see King Agrippa and his daughter visiting Festus. Agrippa wants to hear what Paul has to say…

Read verses 23-27

Think!

Paul had another opportunity to tell people about Jesus! What opportunities do you have to share your faith with people?

_____

_____

_____

Pray!

Ask God to give you great opportunities to tell people about Jesus. Ask Him for the guts to actually do it!

44

Acts
26 v 1-32

WEIRD WORDS

Sect
Religious group

Fulfilled
Come true

Earnestly
Seriously and devotedly

Saints/Lord's people
Christians

Blaspheme
Speak against God

Kick against the goads
It means: "Stop trying to resist me!"

Sanctified
Set apart to serve God

Repent
Turn away from sinful ways

Get Agrippa!

Imagine that you've been locked in prison for 2 years, even though you've done nothing wrong.

In the thought bubble, write how you'd feel.

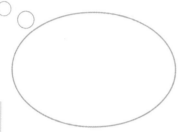

It would be really easy to feel sorry for yourself. Maybe even blame God. But Paul didn't do any of that.

Cross out all the Fs, Hs and Ks to find out what Paul did.

F H H C O H F N T K K I N H U H H
E D K F H T E K K L F F L I N K H
G P F F E H O F F P K H L E A F F
H B O U H K T J E K K F S U S H H

C_____

_____

_____

Paul had been accused of loads of bad stuff by some Jewish trouble-makers. He ended up having to defend himself in front of the very important King Agrippa. So Paul told the king how he'd become a Christian!

Read Acts 26 v 1-32

It's long, so as you read it, write in the box some of the great things Paul said to the king.

Paul was brave. He wanted to tell everyone about Jesus. He wanted everyone to become a Christian.

Pray!

Ask God to give you the same courage and enthusiasm to tell people about Jesus.

Storm troopers

**Acts
27 v 1-26**

Paul the prisoner is now being sent on a ship to Emperor Caesar in Rome.

Sounds boring?

No chance! Get ready for an action-packed, stormy trip...

WEIRD WORDS

Centurion
Commander in the Roman army

Lee
Side of the island protected from the wind

Graciously
Giving them more than they deserved

Read Acts 27 v 1-12

and find some of the places Paul's prison boat sailed past.

```
B  F  R  C  I  L  I  C  I  A
P  A  M  P  H  Y  L  I  A  V
Y  I  D  N  L  O  G  P  S  U
C  R  E  T  E  D  J  K  I  M
X  H  F  Q  U  C  X  T  A  C
S  A  Z  O  S  I  D  O  N  Y
N  V  H  O  Q  A  S  V  X  P
B  E  C  R  Y  R  Z  F  B  R
C  N  I  D  U  S  H  V  A  U
E  S  J  M  Y  R  A  L  K  S
```

A_____

S_____

C_____

C_____

P_____

M_____

C_____

C_____

F_____ H_____

Paul warned the sailors that the seas would become dangerous, but they ignored him.

Read verses 13-20

The sailors tried to get the ship through the fierce storm, using every trick they knew. Eventually they gave up all hope of being saved. They had done everything they could to save the ship... except turn to God for help!

Read verses 21-26

Paul told the men that he belonged to God and served Him (v23). Because Paul lived for God, he had got to know God better. He knew that he could trust God to keep His promises. Paul knew that God was far more powerful than a storm!

Think!

Write down some of the things that scare you (loneliness, terrorism, family problems).

_____

_____

_____

God is much more powerful than any of these things!

Pray!

Ask God to help you trust Him to look after you, no matter what you have to go through in life.

What a wreck!

**Acts
27 v 27-44**

*Paul is a
prisoner on
a ship sailing
to Italy that's
been hit by a
furious storm.
The sailors think
they will all die.*

Read Acts 27 v 27-38

Some of the soldiers tried to escape
but were stopped. Paul encouraged
them all to eat one last meal for
extra strength.

And he thanked God even though
they were close to death. Paul still
trusted God to rescue them!

Read verses 39-44

The soldiers wanted to kill all the
prisoners (including Paul) to stop
them escaping. But what had God
promised them earlier?

Fill in the missing vowels please.

N_t _n_ _f
y_ _ w_ll b_ l_st.
nly th sh_p w_ll
b_ d_str_y_d (v22)

Wow!

NOTHING stops God's plans! He
always keeps His promises!

God has plans for all His people.
And those plans won't be stopped.

*Fill in the gaps from **Jeremiah 29
v 11-13**.*

I kn_w th_ pl_ns I
h_v_ f_r y_ _: pl_ns
t_ pr_sp_r y_ _, n_t
t_ h_rm y_ _, t_
g_v_ y_ _ h_p_
_nd a f_t_r_.

Y_ _ w_ll c_m_
_nd pr_y
t_ m_ _nd I w_ll
l_st_n t_ y_ _.

Y_ _ w_ll
s_ _k m_ _nd f_nd
m_ wh_n y_ _
s_ _k m_ w_th _ll
y_ _r h_ _rt.

Try learning one of these verses!

Pray!

Thank God that He always keeps
His promises. Thank Him that
nothing can stop His perfect
plans.

WEIRD WORDS

Took soundings
Measured the depth
of the sea using a
weight on a long line

Stern
Back of the ship

Bow
Front of the ship

Rudders
Used to steer the
ship

Hoisted
Raised up

Viper smile off his face

**Acts
28 v 1-10**

The ship has been smashed to pieces, but all the crew are safe. God has kept His promise to rescue Paul and everyone on the ship.

WEIRD WORDS

Brushwood
Twigs and sticks

Justice
A fake goddess

Estate
Buildings and land

Hospitably
Welcomingly

Dysentery
Really really bad diarrhoea

Furnished
Gave us

Read Acts 28 v 1-6

It must have been a huge relief to escape a shipwreck and then to meet such kind, friendly people.

Cross out any wrong answers to complete the story.

**Paul threw some wood/coal/ burgers on the fire and a scorpion/anteater/snake bit into his leg/hand/hotdog. The people thought Paul must be a robber/murderer/ chef and expected him to scream/cook/die.
They thought that although he'd escaped from the sea/ prison/anteater, he was getting the punishment he deserved. Paul was grumpy/ in agony/not harmed, so they decided he must be a magician/zookeeper/god!**

These people didn't realise that the miracle was from the only true God, who protects His people. But this doesn't mean that Christians never get hurt.

It does show that God always makes sure that things work out for His good purposes. Nothing will stop Him working out His plans for us!

Read verses 7-10

Paul stayed with Peter/Pablo/ Publius, the chief official of the island. Paul healed his mother/father/puppy. After that, everyone on the island who was well/sick/silly came to Paul and was killed/ curried/cured.

On the ship in the storm, the situation seemed terrible. Why would God allow that to happen? But God kept His promise, kept them safe and took Paul to Malta where he healed loads of people!

Wow!
Sometimes we don't understand where God is taking our lives and why. But we can trust that He will look after His people because His plans are perfect.

Pray!

Thank God that He is always in control, even when we can barely believe it. Ask Him to use your life to serve Him in surprising ways.

Man of hope and glory

45

**Acts
28 v 11-20**

After three months in sunny Malta, Paul and the prison ship finally left to continue their journey to Rome in Italy.

WEIRD WORDS

Alexandrian
From Alexandria in Egypt

Figurehead
Large carved wooden figure at the front of a ship

Brothers and sisters
Christians

Bound
Tied up

Read Acts 28 v 11-16

Paul was so happy to meet these Christians. They had travelled a long way to meet him.

Action!

How can you make an effort to meet other Christians' needs? (Talk to new people at church? Help Christians with chores?)

_____

_____

Read verses 17-20

Complete Paul's story by finding the 10 missing words in the wordsearch and putting them into the right spaces.

V	L	J	E	W	S	C	O	R
T	N	E	C	O	N	N	I	G
D	A	R	R	E	S	T	E	D
C	N	U	F	N	S	J	B	N
A	G	S	A	C	Y	V	E	U
E	R	A	P	H	L	R	Q	O
S	Y	L	P	A	X	N	A	B
A	D	E	E	I	A	U	Z	K
R	O	M	A	N	S	H	J	P
S	P	O	L	S	P	N	U	K

Paul was a_____ in J_____ (v17).
He was handed over to the R_____ (v17).
The J_____ were so a_____ that the Roman governor was too scared to let Paul go, even though he knew Paul was i_____.
Paul had to a_____ to C_____ (v19).
He was b_____ in c_____ (v20).

Why did Paul put up with being treated badly by his own people?

Because of the h__p__ of __sr__ __l (v20)

Who was this hope that Paul was talking about? The only hope for Jewish people, the only hope for you and me?

J__ __ __ __

Think & pray!

Like Paul, are you ready to tell people about Jesus, whatever hassle it gets you into? If you are, tell God right now and ask Him to help you.

The final acts

Judea
Where Jews were originally from

Sect
Religious group. They meant Christianity.

Law of Moses/ The Prophets
Old Testament

Perceiving
Understanding

Calloused
Hardened

Salvation
Rescue

Gentiles
Non-Jewish people

Hindrance
Difficulty

Paul is telling loads of Jewish people about Jesus. Do you think they'll listen to him?

Yes/No _____

Read Acts 28 v 21-27

Some of them believed Paul.

But most of them refused to listen.

They refused to look at the evidence that Jesus was their King.

Read verses 28-31

These Jewish people refused to turn to Jesus. What was the result?

Write down every second letter to find out. Start with the top G and go clockwise.

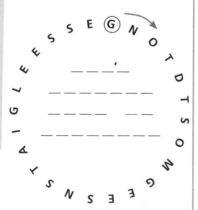

____ ' ____

____ ____

____ ____ ____

Wow! 1

The Jews were God's special people, chosen to serve Him. But many of them refused to live for God. They refused to believe in Jesus. So they wouldn't get to live with Him for ever.

Wow! 2

Now, God's message isn't just for Jewish people. It's for EVERYONE! Anyone can trust in Jesus and have their sins forgiven. Anyone can choose to live for Him.

Pray!

Thank God that His amazing message, of Jesus dying for us, is for EVERYONE.

47 The real Jesus

Today we get back to John's story of Jesus' life.

An amazing miracle sets the scene for the whole chapter...

WEIRD WORDS

Rabbi
Teacher

Read John 9 v 1-3

and unjumble the anagrams.

This guy was born

_____. Jesus'
d i n b l

followers wanted to know

whose _____ had caused
i n s

his blindness.

Jesus said that it wasn't sin that caused the man to be blind. This man was blind so that people would see the

_____ of _____
k r o w   o d G

in his life.

Jesus was about to do something amazing in this man's life!

Read verses 4-5

What did Jesus say next?

We must do the

_____ of Him who
r o w k

_____ me.
t e n s

While Jesus was still on earth, He and His disciples served God in everything they did.

_____ is coming
t h i n g

when _____
e n n o o

can work.

I am the _____
g h i l t

of the _____.
d r o w l

Wow!

People who don't know Jesus are blind. They don't realise they need Jesus to forgive them for their sins. They need to turn to Him before it's too late. Jesus is the light showing up the sin in our lives and He shows us the way to be forgiven.

Read verses 6-7

Jesus put _____ mixed
d u m

with _____ on the man's
t i p s

_____ and told him
y e e s

to wash in the

_____ of _____.
l o o p   a m S o i l

The man trusted Jesus, obeyed Him and his sight was cured! If people obey Jesus and trust Him, they can have their sins forgiven!

Pray!

Thank Jesus that He shows up our sin and shows us the way to have our sin forgiven!

48

Blind fury

John
9 v 8-17

Jesus has just healed a man who was blind from birth.

Imagine the excitement when people realise that he can see!

WEIRD WORDS

Pharisees
Religious leaders who were against Jesus

Prophet
Messenger from God

Signs
Miracles

Read John 9 v 8-12

Isn't that the blind guy who used to beg?

It's just someone who looks like him.

It's true, I am the man who was blind!

So how were your eyes healed???

Jesus did it!

Read verses 13-17

What did some of the Pharisees say against Jesus? (Fill in the vowels.)

H__ __s n_t fr_m
G_d, f_r h_
d__ _s n_t k___p
th_ S__bb__th (v16)

The Sabbath

It was the special Jewish day of the week for resting and worshipping God. One of the 10 Commandments says: "Remember the Sabbath day by keeping it holy".

Question Time!

1. Is it right to be concerned about keeping God's commandments?
YES/NO _____

God is, so we should be too.

2. So had Jesus disobeyed God?
YES/NO _____

God's law doesn't say it's wrong to do good on the Sabbath!

What did some of the others say?

H__w c_n a
s_nn_r p_rf_rm
s_ch s_gns? (v16)

Maybe they realised that only God could do such amazing things. And so Jesus must have been sent by God!

The ex-blind man thought that Jesus was just a prophet. He didn't realise that Jesus was God's Son.

Think & pray!

Who do YOU think Jesus is? If you believe that He is God's Son, is there anything you want to say to Him right now?

Blind bravery

Jesus has amazingly healed a blind man. But the Pharisees still won't believe that He is God's Son!

WEIRD WORDS

He is of age
Old enough to speak for himself

Acknowledged
Believed

The Messiah
God's promised Rescuer

Synagogue
Where people met to learn from the Scriptures

Sinner
Someone who disobeys God

Read John 9 v 18-23

Who did the Jewish leaders send for?

the blind man's pal ☐
the blind man's parakeet ☐
the blind man's parents ☐

The man's parents were...

afraid of the Jewish leaders ☐
afraid of Jesus ☐
afraid of jellyfish ☐

The Jewish leaders wouldn't accept that Jesus was sent by God. They even threatened to throw people out of the synagogue if they said that Jesus was the Messiah. That meant they'd be cut off from their friends and become outsiders. So the man's parents kept quiet out of fear.

Wow!

Of course, Jesus **is** the Messiah — the perfect king who came to rescue God's people!

Read verses 24-25

The Pharisees tried to get the man to say Jesus was...

a saviour ☐
a sinner ☐
a swimmer ☐

But unlike his parents, the man was brave enough to stand up to the cruel Jewish leaders.

He wouldn't speak against Jesus, even though it would mean rejection, and losing friends.

Think!

Ever feel under pressure to speak against Jesus? Will you stand up for Him even though it might mean rejection?

Pray!

Ask God to give you the courage to speak up for Jesus, even when it means getting a hard time for it.

For the free e-booklet *How do I show I'm a Christian?* email discover@thegoodbook.co.uk or check out www.thegoodbook.co.uk/contact-us to find our UK mailing address.

Blinding truth

**John
9 v 26-34**

*The Pharisees
are still quizzing
the ex-blind
man about
Jesus.*

*Let's listen
in on their
conversation...
(and then fill
in the missing
first letters of
words!)*

WEIRD WORDS

Disciples
Followers, people
who were taught
by Jesus

Godly person
Someone who
serves God rather
than living for
themselves

His will
What God wants
us/them to do

Steeped in sin
Full of sin

Read John 9 v 26-27

__hat __id he do to
__ou? How did Jesus
open your __yes?

I have __lready __old
__ou, but you won't
listen! __hy do you
__ant to __ear it
__gain? Do you want to
become his __isciples?

This really annoyed the Pharisees.
They were furious!

Read verses 28-29

We are __isciples
of __oses. We
__now __hat __od
__poke to __oses,
but we don't even
know where Jesus
__omes __rom!

They were making **excuses** for not
believing that Jesus was God's Son.
They ignored the fact that He had
healed this man. And they ignored
the amazing things Jesus said.

Think!

Do you make excuses for
not believing Jesus? Excuses for not
living for Him?

Read verses 30-34

Jesus cured my
blindness. We __now
that __od doesn't
__isten to __inners. God
listens to people who
obey Him. If this __an
was not __rom __od,
he wouldn't have been
able to heal me!

Brilliant! This man worked out that
Jesus must be from God, because
Jesus could do things that only God
could do. Sadly, the Pharisees still
refused to believe the evidence!

Action!

Do you believe that Jesus is from
God? That He is God's Son? Keep
reading the evidence in the Bible
and make up your own mind.

Pray!

Ask God to help you discover the
truth about Jesus.

51

John
9 v 35-41

The Pharisees threw the ex-blind man out of the temple.

He had become an outcast.

So Jesus went to find him...

Blind faith

Read John 9 v 35-37

Fill in the amazing words to reveal the truth about Jesus.

> Do you believe in the
> S_____ of M_____?

The Son of Man is the name Jesus called Himself. Jesus is God, but He became a man so that He could die for us and rescue us from our wrong ways.

Read verse 38

> The man said "I
> b_____" and he
> worshipped Jesus.

That's the right way to respond to Jesus the Rescuer. To tell Him that you believe in Him. And to worship Him and serve Him with your whole life.

Read verses 39-41

> I have come into the
> w_____ so that the
> b_____ will s_____
> and those who s_____ will
> become b_____

Confused? Then listen up...

The Pharisees thought they could see. They thought they knew the truth about God. But they didn't, because they refused to see that Jesus is God. So they wouldn't have their sins forgiven by Jesus.

Some people realise they are blind and that they need Jesus to rescue them from their blind, sinful ways. And Jesus will, if they ask Him to.

Think & pray!

There are two choices. Believe in Jesus and worship Him with your life. Or refuse to let Him rescue you. Which will YOU choose? Ask God to help you make the right choice.

For a free e-booklet called *Why did Jesus come?* email discover@thegoodbook.co.uk or check out www.thegoodbook.co.uk/contact-us to find our UK mailing address.

52

**John
10 v 1-6**

Feeling sheepish today?

If you follow Jesus, you should be!

In at the sheep end

Read John 10 v 1-6

Baffled? Don't worry, verse 6 says you're not the only one!

Sheep Facts!

In Bible times, sheep from different flocks were kept in one big sheep pen or sheepfold (see the pic on day 53). The only entrance was a gate. A gatekeeper stayed with the sheep to stop them being stolen. Sheep from the same flock only followed the voice of their shepherd. No one else could lead them.

Use the word pool to fill in the gaps. Watch out for red sheep, er, herrings!

> Bible   speaks
>
> obeying   wolves
>
> sheep   lamb chops
>
> live   words

Jesus s_____ to us in the B_____. His s_____ follow Him by o_____ His w_____, wanting to l_____ like He did.

Pray!

Ask God to help you to really follow His Son, Jesus. To obey His words in the Bible. And to live only for Him.

WEIRD WORDS

**Gatekeeper/
Watchman**

Like a security guard, making sure no one steals the sheep

Jesus is the shepherd.

His followers (Christians) are the sheep.

Ungodly religious leaders are the robbers.

Religious leaders (like the Pharisees) tried to lead people away from God (v1).

But true followers of Jesus will follow only Him (v4). He shows them the way to live their lives. They won't follow anyone else.

For the free e-booklet *How do I grow as a Christian?* email
discover@thegoodbook.co.uk
or check out
www.thegoodbook.co.uk/contact-us
to find our UK mailing address.

Gate expectations

Yesterday we read that Christians are like sheep who follow their shepherd — Jesus Christ.

Today, Jesus describes Himself slightly differently.

Read John 10 v 7-10

Jesus is the shepherd.

But He's also the g_____

How many ways into the sheepfold are there?

What does Jesus call other people who claim to be the way to God (v8)?

t_ _ _ _ _ _

and

r_ _ _ _ _ _

What do they do (v10)?

s_ _ _ _ _,

k_ _ _ and

d_ _ _ _ _ _

Jesus is the **ONLY** way to God. Anyone else who claims to be the way to God is lying and will lead people to eternal death in hell.

But what two amazing claims does Jesus make?

1. Whoever enters through me will be

s_ _ _ _ _! (v9)

Have you been saved from sin by Jesus? Has He forgiven your wrongs?

YES/NO _____

2. I have come that they may have l_ _ _ (v10)

Can you look forward to everlasting life with Jesus?

YES/NO _____

Pray!

Jesus promises to look after anyone who turns to Him. To give them everything they need! If He has saved you, then you've got loads to thank Him for right now! Go on!

Think!

Maybe you haven't turned to Jesus to be forgiven. Maybe you're not sure if you'll live with Jesus for ever.
For a free fact sheet on *How to become a Christian* email discover@thegoodbook.co.uk or check out www.thegoodbook.co.uk/contact-us to find our UK mailing address.

WEIRD WORDS

Pasture
Somewhere safe to rest and be fed

The Good Shepherd

54

**John
10 v 11-15**

*We're still
thinking about
sheep.*

*Mmm... no, not
lamb chops!*

Christians!

WEIRD WORDS

Hired hand
Someone hired
to look after the
sheep. He doesn't
really care about
the sheep.

Read John 10 v 11-13

*Fill in the spaces, using the **shaded
blocks**, please!*

sheep	destroyed	died

the good shepherd	devil

Jesus	gone to hell

wolf	followers	wolf

destroyed	Jesus

the good shepherd	devil

_____

saved his _____ from
being _____ by
the _____. Anyone
else would have run away
and left them to face the
_____. They would
have all _____. But

_____

was willing to die to
rescue them!

So what's that all about???

*Do you remember who the sheep
and shepherd really are? (See day
52.) Now fill in the spaces using the
white blocks.*

_____ saved His
_____ from
being _____ by
the _____. Anyone
else would have left them
to face the _____.
They would have all

_____.

But _____ was willing
to die to rescue them!

Read through that again. It's
amazing!

Now read verses 14-15

Wow!

Jesus died to rescue anyone who
trusts Him to save them! And we
can get to know Jesus really really
well. We can be close to Jesus,
just as He is close to His Father,
God!
If you want to be Jesus' friend,
tell Him right now...

Flock tactics

John
10 v 16-18

How big is your family?

_____

_____

_____

_____

_____

In today's Bible bit, Jesus says that all Christians are in one HUGE family…

Read John 10 v 16

> **What's Jesus talking about???**

Jesus was talking to **Jewish** people. They were God's chosen people and thought they'd be the only ones who would be with God forever.

"I have other sheep that are not of this sheepfold"

Jesus is saying that He hasn't come just to save Jews from their sins. He has come to save **non-Jews** too!

"There shall be one flock"

There are now believers all over the world, living very different lives. But they've all been saved by Jesus!

They are all one big family!

WEIRD WORDS

Own accord
Own choice

Authority
Power

Pray!

Pray for (and thank God for) your Christian brothers and sisters all over the world. Especially those…

– in countries where there are very few Christians (Albania, Turkey, Japan)

– in countries where Christians are persecuted (Iran, China, Syria, Iraq)

Read verses 17-18

Wow!

Jesus chose to die on the cross to take the punishment we deserve for the wrong stuff we've done.

And He had power to rise again to beat sin and death and the devil!

He did all of that for us!

Prayer action!

Grab some spare paper. Write a prayer to thank Jesus for all that He has done for YOU. Then spend time talking to Him, using that prayer.

Short sheep shock

John
10 v 19-30

In today's Bible bit, people are still arguing about who Jesus is...

WEIRD WORDS

Demon-possessed
Has an evil spirit inside him

Festival of Dedication
Special feast for God's temple in Jerusalem

Colonnade
A covered passageway with lots of tall stone columns either side of it

Works
Miracles

Perish
Die

Read John 10 v 19-24

These people think that Jesus is either from the **devil** or from **God**. Some of them want to know if Jesus really is the Christ who has come to rescue them.

Read verses 25-27

*What **evidence** had they seen that Jesus is the Christ?*

Go back one letter to find out.

_ _ _ _ _ _ _ _ (v25)
N J S B D M F T

_ _ _ _   _ _ _ _ _
X I B U   K F T V T

_ _ _ _ (v27)
T B J E

These people had seen loads of evidence that Jesus is the great Rescuer. But they still wouldn't become His followers (sheep).

Read verses 27-29

What three things does Jesus promise to people who do follow Him?

1. _   _ _ _ _
   J   L O P X

   _ _ _ _ (v27)
   U I F N

   They are His friends!

2. _ _ _ _   _ _ _ _
   H J W F   U I F N

   _ _ _ _ _ _ _
   F U F S O B M

   _ _ _ _ (v28)
   M J G F

   They'll live with Jesus for ever!

3. _ _   _ _ _
   O P   P O F

   _ _ _   _ _ _ _ _
   D B O   T O B U D I

   _ _ _ _ (v29)
   U I F N

   No one can take them away from Jesus!

Read verse 30

4. _   _ _ _   _ _ _
   J   B O E   U I F

   _ _ _ _ _
   G B U I F S

   _ _ _   _ _ _
   B S F   P O F

   Jesus is God! We can be friends with God!

Pray!

Read through those four things again, thanking and praising Jesus.

**John
10 v 31-42**

Yesterday, Jesus said:

> **I and the Father are one.**

Blasphemy blast

Read John 10 v 31-33

Jesus claimed to be **God**. The punishment for blasphemy was death. Finally, they had an excuse to kill Him!

But Jesus gave two reasons why He could claim to be God...

Read verses 34-36

1. The Bible

In the Old Testament (Psalm 82 v 6), God called certain people "gods".

He meant that they had been chosen by God Himself to serve Him. Yet Jesus had been sent specially by His Father God to rescue the world! Couldn't they see how much more important Jesus was???

Think!

Do people ever quiz you about Jesus and Christian stuff? Here are some great verses about Jesus that are worth learning: John 3 v 16
                    John 3 v 36
                    John 14 v 6

Read verses 37-38

2. What Jesus did

Jesus is saying: "If the way I act is any different from the way God acts, don't believe that I'm God." But Jesus is perfect. Jesus is God.

Action!

Does the way that you act show that you're a follower of Jesus? What can you do to live more like Jesus? To live God's way?

_____

_____

_____

WEIRD WORDS

Blasphemy
Claiming to be God

Law/Scripture
Old Testament

The Jordan
A large river

Baptising
Dunking people under water as a sign that they were now living for God

Read verses 39-42

Jesus escaped the people who wouldn't believe Him. He went to people who believed Him and wanted to live God's way.

Do YOU believe Jesus' claims?

James: Fantastic faith

**James
1 v 1-4**

Today we begin reading a great letter!

It's all about how to live for God in a world that doesn't want us to.

WEIRD WORDS

Twelve tribes
Jewish Christians

Trials
Tough times

Faith
Trust in God

Perseverance
Sticking at something and not giving up

Read James 1 v 1

Who wrote this letter?

J_____. He was a

s_____ of God and

of Jesus Christ (v1).

Many people reckon that this was Jesus' brother, James. But the most important thing about him is that he **served God**.

James wrote this letter to Jewish Christians around the world. It told them how their faith in Jesus should be obvious in everything they do. We can learn loads from this letter too!

Think!

What do you think or say when life seems too hard?

_____

_____

_____

Read verse 2

What does James tell Christians to do when they face tough times?

That's not our normal reaction to problems, is it?! But God often uses tough times to teach us things and to help us grow closer to Him. So we can even thank God for problems we have!

Read verses 3-4

Wow!

James says that hard times teach us to stick with God and tough it out. They help us to live more for Him. That's why Christians should praise God even when things go wrong!

Pray!

Ask God to help you stick with Him through tough times. Ask Him to use those times to bring you closer to Him.

For a free fact sheet on *FACING TOUGH TIMES*, email discover@thegoodbook.co.uk or check out www.thegoodbook.co.uk/contact-us to find our UK mailing address.

Wise and wonderful

Brainstorm!

*What do you
think WISDOM
means?*

_____

_____

_____

_____

_____

_____

WEIRD WORDS

Double minded
Can't make his mind
up whether to trust
God

Unstable
Not a very strong
Christian

*What does the Bible say about
wisdom? Find **Job 28 v 28** and
write it out.*

_____

_____

_____

_____

_____

Wow!

Being wise doesn't mean just
knowing loads. True wisdom is
giving God the respect He deserves.
Living God's way. Turning away
from sinful ways. That's really wise!

Read James 1 v 5

Life can seem like a maze
sometimes, with different ways to
go and problems to face.

*So what should we do if we want to
make decisions that please God? Fill
in the first letter of each word.*

__f __ny __f __ou
__acks __isdom, __ou
__hould __sk __od (v5)

Ask God to give you wisdom and He
will! He will help you to face tough
times, to make wise decisions, and
to live in a way that pleases Him!

Read verses 6-8

*When we ask God for things (like
wisdom), what should we do?*

_____ and

not _____ (v6)

God can do anything! And He
loves to give things like wisdom to
His people. We can trust Him and
believe that He will answer our
prayers. Maybe not always in the
way we expect, but He will answer
our prayers.

Pray!

What decisions or problems do
you need help with?

_____

_____

_____

Ask God to help you be wise
in these situations. Ask Him for
wisdom to live His way.

For richer or poorer

**James
1 v 9-12**

Andy is loaded. He gets £50 a week pocket money and owns loads of video games.

Anna gets 50p and has nothing to entertain her except second-hand books.

WEIRD WORDS

Humble circumstances
Having no money

Blessed
Given great things by God

Perseveres
Keeps going

Crown of life
The great prize! Eternal life!

Out of Andy and Anna, who's rich and who's poor?

The answer seems obvious, but James disagrees...

Read James 1 v 9-11

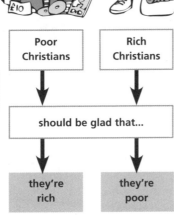

Poor Christians	Rich Christians

should be glad that...

they're rich	they're poor

Has James got it all the wrong way round??? Nope! The white boxes up on the right are true for all Christians, but draw lines to show the best two answers to each question.

How is a poor Christian rich?	How is a rich Christian poor?

Will have eternal life

Knows he's a poor sinner

Knows that in heaven his money is worth nothing

God meets all her needs

It can be really hard being poor. And it can also be hard to live God's way if you've got lots. James has great news for Christians whether they are rich or poor...

Read verse 12

Wow!

If we stick with God through tough times, God promises us the crown of life. That means eternal life. All Christians will one day live with God!

Pray!

Think of a rich Christian you know, and a poor one. Ask God to help them both stick with Him through the different problems they face.

61

**James
1 v 13-16**

In his letter, James has been telling Christians that if they want to live for God, then they will have to cope with tough times.

Tempting offer

It's true! Christians will be hassled for following Jesus.

But we shouldn't use tough times as an excuse to give in to temptation and sin...

Read James 1 v 13-14

Don't blame God when you're tempted to sin! And don't blame anyone else either! It's our fault if we give in and do wrong stuff. We have to say sorry to God, and then get back to living His way.

Read verse 15

and complete the sequence.

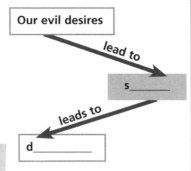

Our evil desires

lead to

s_____

leads to

d_____

Think!

What wrong things are you sometimes tempted to do?

Think of some of your own...

lie to get out of trouble

use bad language

watch things I shouldn't

_____

_____

Read verse 16

We must try to fight temptation. But we're not on our own; we can ask God to help us!

WEIRD WORDS

Evil desire
Wanting to sin

Enticed
Tempted to sin

Conceived
Started to grow, like a tiny baby inside its mother

Wow!

Sin separates us from God. People who choose to live their own sinful way and not God's way will be punished by eternal death in hell. But people who turn their back on sin will have their sins forgiven! Christians still sin sometimes, but they now live more and more for God!

Pray!

Say sorry to God for the stuff you've written under *Think!* Ask God to help you fight the temptation to do these things. And if you give in to them, say sorry again and keep asking God to help you!

Life lessons

James 1 v 17-21

Let's learn some top life lessons from James...

Use the word pool to fill in today's blanks.

accept   angry   evil

Father   good   listen

perfect   rid   save

speak   truth   word

Lesson 1: Good stuff comes from God!

Read James 1 v 17

Every g_____ and
p_____ gift comes
from the F_____ of
the heavenly lights.

What are some of the good things you enjoy?

_____

_____

God made them possible!

Lesson 2: Best present of all!

Read verse 18

God made it possible for
us to become Christians
through the w_____ of
t_____

God has shown us the truth about
Jesus — that if we ask Him to, He
can forgive our sins! That's the best
gift ever! James says that Christians
are really important to God!

Lesson 3: Be quick and slow!

Read verses 19-20

Be quick to l_____,
slow to s_____ and
slow to get a_____.

Great advice! We should **listen**
more to people and show we care
about what they have to say. The
more we **speak**, the more likely
we'll say something we shouldn't.
We should think before we speak,
and that will help us fight the
temptation to get angry.

Lesson 4: Throw it out!

Read verse 21

Get r_____ of bad and
e_____ habits. Humbly
a_____ God's Word,
which can s_____ you.

You can ask God to help you stop
doing wrong stuff. And try to
obey His Word (the Bible), which
He has lovingly given us.

Pray!

Read through the four lessons.
Which one do you need most
help with? Lesson _____
Talk to God about it right now.

Mirror mirror on the wall

**James
1 v 22-25**

*Go and have a
look at yourself
in the mirror.*

Go on!

*Maybe a quick
brush of your
hair, and you'll
be fine...*

WEIRD WORDS

**The word/
perfect law**
God's Word, the
Bible

Intently
Giving it great
attention

Blessed
God will be with
him and give him
far more than he
deserves

That's the way we often use mirrors.
A quick peek to make sure we're
OK, and then we can forget about
how we look. But James tells us
that's not the way to use the Bible.

Read James 1 v 22-25

Put v22 into your own words.

Just reading the Bible isn't enough.
We've got to do what it says!

The Bible is like a mirror...

1. Do you look in it?

You obviously do read the Bible, or
you wouldn't be reading *Discover!*
But do you look carefully in it, to see
what it shows about you?

2. How closely do you look?

Do you spend ages examining
yourself in the mirror? A close
examination is what the Bible
deserves. Not seeing how fast you
can finish your Bible notes, but
a long hard look at what God is
saying. After reading the Bible, ask
yourself: *What have I learned today?*

3. What will you do about
what you see?

The Bible often has a challenging
message for us. Do you just read
what God's Word says and then
forget about it? **Or will you do
something about it?**

Read verses 22-25 again

Action!

Every time you look quickly
in the mirror, remember that's not
how to read your Bible!

Examine it closely!

Then do what it says!

Pray!

Ask God to help you learn from
the Bible. Ask Him to speak to
you through the Bible. And ask
Him to help you do what it says.

Real religion

James
1 v 26-27

*Would you describe yourself as a **religious** person?*

YES/NO _____

WEIRD WORDS

Religious
Devoted to God

Tight rein
Control

Pure and faultless
Perfect — good enough for God

Polluted by the world
Letting sin affect our lives, so that we sin too

Today's missing words can be found in the wordsearch.

```
R  E  P  U  R  E  N  R  T  A
D  E  O  R  P  H  A  N  S  L
E  P  L  Q  X  F  T  B  T  J
C  Q  L  I  R  D  H  T  P  W
E  O  U  K  G  S  B  O  M  I
I  J  T  C  H  I  W  N  G  D
V  G  E  Y  C  O  O  G  U  O
I  M  D  M  K  P  R  U  Z  W
N  WO  R  T  H  L  E  S  S
G  U  F  B  S  L  D  A  V  G
```

Read James 1 v 26

If anyone thinks they are

r_____

but doesn't control

their t_____, they

are d_____

themselves. Their religion is

w_____ (v26).

Tip 1: Tame that tongue!

If we're serious about serving God, we'll want to cut out bad language. And we'll try to stop saying nasty things about other people.

Read James 1 v 27

God says that p_____
religion is looking after

o_____ and

w_____ (v27).

Tip 2: Care for people!

James says that religiously serving God means caring for people who are having a rotten time.

Who do you know who would value your care and friendship?

_____

_____

Don't be p_____ by
the w_____ (v27).

Tip 3: Fight pollution!

If we give in to sin and temptation, we are letting sin pollute us, and get a grip on us.

What sins do you need to keep fighting?

_____

_____

_____

_____

Pray!

Read the three tips again. Spend time on each one, asking God to help you with it.

Favour flavour

James
2 v 1-9

WEIRD WORDS

Glorious
Brilliant, perfect, deserving glory

Discriminated
Shown favouritism

Rich in faith
Trusting God

Inherit the kingdom
Get to be part of God's kingdom!

Exploiting
Taking advantage of them

Blaspheming
Saying bad things against God

Noble name
God, who is holy and perfect

Convicted
Found guilty

What's your favourite food?

What's your favourite movie?

Where's your favourite place?

It's good to have favourite things. But James says don't show favouritism to people...

Read James 2 v 1-4

Who would you sit next to in church?

 **OR**

Back in James' time, rich people were often treated with great respect in church, yet a poor person might not even get a seat!

Read verses 5-7

The poor will be rich! God often chooses poor, weak, unknown people to serve Him in great ways (v5). Jesus spent loads of time with people who were poor and in need. So we shouldn't look down on people who are worse off than us.

Action!

We can give time and help to people who are in need.

Who did you write down in Tip 2 yesterday?

_____

So what are you going to do?

_____

_____

_____

_____

Read verses 8-9

Neighbours doesn't just mean next-door neighbours. It means **everyone** we meet. We should show love to all of them, not just the ones we find it easiest to get on with.

Pray!

Ask God to help you show love to people you wouldn't normally hang out with.

**James
2 v 10-13**

I only broke a bit of the window!

I don't think your mum would be very happy with that excuse!

WEIRD WORDS

Adultery
Cheating on your husband or wife

Judgment without mercy
God won't forgive those who reject Him

Merciful
Showing forgiveness

Don't forget to forgive

And neither is God...

> Yes, I lied at school, but I didn't KILL anyone...

Read James 2 v 10-11

Tick the box which best describes you

I'm a good person ☐
I'm not as bad as some ☐
I do a few wrong things ☐
I sin all the time ☐

James says that if you disobey God just once, or lots of times, you still deserve to be punished.

Read verses 12-13

By what law are we judged? (v12)

The law that

_____

_____

Wow!

Even though we are guilty of disobeying God, there is FREE forgiveness for everyone who trusts in Jesus. They'll be free from sin ruling their lives.

But there is no freedom for people who don't want His forgiveness. They'll get the punishment they deserve.

If you're a Christian, God has forgiven all your sins! So should you show forgiveness to other people?

YES/NO _____

We all *deserve* to be punished for sinning against God. Yet if we are followers of Jesus, God forgives us. In the same way, we should *forgive* people who have done us wrong, Even if they don't deserve to be forgiven!

Action!

Who do you need to show forgiveness and love towards?

_____

_____

_____

Now ask God to help you do it!

Action stations

**James
2 v 14-19**

How much do
you know about
Christianity?

Loads?

Quite a lot?

Not much?

It's time to put
you to the test...

WEIRD WORDS

Faith
Here it means belief
in God

Deeds
Things you do that
show you love God

**Brother and
sister**
Other Christians

Demons
Evil spirits

EXAM – CHRISTIAN FAITH

*1. Who did God send to die
in your place?*

a) No one ☐

b) Moses ☐

c) Jesus ☐

*2. Which is the only way to
get to heaven?*

a) Going to church ☐

b) Trusting Jesus to
forgive you ☐

c) Living a good life ☐

I hope you'd score well in this test!
But **knowing** lots about God and
Christianity doesn't make you a
Christian!

Read James 2 v 14-19

James says that just believing that
God exists isn't enough. Even
demons believe that — and they
don't serve God!

James says that you can tell if
someone's really a Christian by what
they do.

Wow!

People who've truly had their sins
forgiven by God let their faith affect
their whole lives. It's no good saying
you believe in God, but carrying on
stealing stuff, or refusing to honour
your parents. We have to put our
faith into action!

James is **NOT** saying that doing
good deeds makes you a Christian.
Only trusting Jesus to forgive you
is enough. But James says that real
faith in Jesus will lead to many good
actions. People will see that Jesus is
a big part of your life!

Action!

What action do you need to take, to
live more for Jesus?

1. _____

   _____

2. _____

   _____

3. _____

   _____

Pray!

Ask God to help you do those
things. Ask Him to help you live in
a way that brings glory to Him.

James
2 v 20-26

Rahab

On the faith of it

Yesterday James told us that we need to put our faith in Jesus to be rescued from sin. But we need to turn that faith into **action** and start living God's way. By the way, have you started on your three action tasks yet?

James gives us two examples of people whose **faith** in God was shown by their **actions**.

Read James 2 v 20-24

and use the backwards word pool to fill in the gaps.

> bahaR   caasI   epacse
>
> seips   snoitca   suoethgir
>
> htiaf   maharbA   ratIa

1. Abraham

A_____ was considered r_____ when he offered his son, I_____, on the a_____ (v21). His f_____ and a_____ were working together (v22).

Abraham obeyed God's command to kill his son, Isaac (it's OK, God stopped Abraham doing it!). Abraham proved his faith in God by obeying God.

Read verses 25-26

2. Rahab

R_____ had not lived a good life. Yet she showed that she had faith in God by hiding Israelite s_____ and helping them to e_____ (v25).

Both Abraham and Rahab showed they had real faith in God by **obeying Him**. Christians are different from everyone else. They want to please God and not just please themselves.

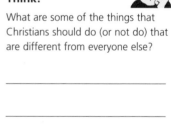

Think!
What are some of the things that Christians should do (or not do) that are different from everyone else?

_____

_____

_____

Think & pray!

Is there proof in your life that you have faith in Jesus? How are the three tasks you wrote down yesterday going? Ask God to help you with them.

More from James in the next issue of *Discover*!

WEIRD WORDS

Righteous
Living God's way

Altar
Table where gifts to God were put

Scripture
The Old Testament

Rahab the prostitute
Before she trusted God, Rahab was sinful and was paid to sleep with people

Justified
Shown to be forgiven by God

Exodus: God is great!

**Exodus
16 v 1-3**

Today we rejoin Moses and the Israelites in the desert.

Can you remember what's happened so far?

WEIRD WORDS

Elim
Nice place with shady trees and fresh water

Aaron
Moses' brother. He often spoke to the Israelites for Moses.

Assembly
All the Israelites

Exodus — Story so far

God's people, the Israelites, were slaves in Egypt. God used Moses (and 10 plagues) to rescue them. But Pharaoh and the Egyptians chased the Israelites. God parted the Red Sea so the Israelites could walk through safely. Then He drowned the evil Egyptian army. Now God's people are in the desert…

Read Exodus 16 v 1-3

What did the Israelites say? Fill in the vowels (aeiou) please.

> If only the L__rd had k__ll__d us in __gypt! There we s__t round p__ts of m__ __t and ate all the f__ __d we w__nt__d, but you have brought us into this d__s__rt to st__rv__ us all to d__ __th.

They were starving and blamed Moses and Aaron. They even said it would have been better to have died in Egypt! They had forgotten **God**.

God had rescued them from Egypt! He had parted the Red Sea for them and defeated their enemies! But the Israelites still didn't trust God to look after them. Crazy!

They had forgotten all that God had done for them. They didn't trust Him to keep them alive. Unbelievable! Or is it?

Think!

Do you sometimes forget all the great things God has done for you? Do you forget that He is in control? Do you grumble and forget to TRUST GOD and ask Him to help you?

List some of the great things God has done.

_____

_____

_____

_____

_____

_____

_____

Pray!

God is so great! He looks after His people! So we can trust Him completely. Talk to God right now about things that are on your mind. Thank Him that He is in control and ask Him to help you.

Whole rain bread

Exodus 16 v 4-8

The Israelites were in the desert with no food.

So they started grumbling at Moses and Aaron.

They had forgotten that God was with them, looking after them.

WEIRD WORDS

Glory of the Lord

They will get a glimpse of God's greatness

Amazingly, God didn't punish them for their lack of faith…

Read Exodus 16 v 4-5

They deserved nothing, but God promised to make bread rain down from heaven! God was showing His great love for the Israelites. But He also had other reasons for doing this miracle…

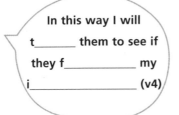

In this way I will t_____ them to see if they f_____ my i_____ (v4)

God's Test

Even more important than a school test! The test to show that they trusted God was whether they obeyed His instructions. (We'll find out if they did in the next few days.)

Wow!

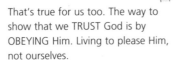

That's true for us too. The way to show that we TRUST God is by OBEYING Him. Living to please Him, not ourselves.

Read verses 6-8

Why else did God do this miracle? Complete Moses' answer.

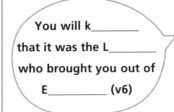

You will k_____ that it was the L_____ who brought you out of E_____ (v6)

God promised to give the Israelites miraculous food so that they would know that He was **their God**, who rescued them from Egypt. Christians have the same God looking after them. He is **their God**!

Action!

How can you obey God more in your everyday life?

_____

_____

_____

Check out 1 John 3 v 23

Pray!

Thank God that He is still the God of His people today, caring for them. Ask God to help you TRUST Him and OBEY Him more in the everyday things you do.

A quail of a time

**Exodus
16 v 9-20**

The Israelites are moaning about having no food.

So God is going to give them food in a miraculous way.

Read Exodus 16 v 9-12

and cross out the wrong answers.

The Lord heard the Israelites' mumbling/grumbling/tumbling (v12).

He promised to give them bread/meat/feet to eat at night and bread/thread/meat in the morning (v12).

After seeing this miracle, the Israelites/Egyptians would know that the Lord was their enemy/God (v12).

Think of some of the things God has done for you. Think of times He has answered prayer. Christians can be confident that **the Lord is their God**!

Read verses 13-18

That evening hail/quail/whales covered the camp, and in the morning there was a layer of snow/dew (v13).

After the dew cleared, thin flakes/snakes/cakes appeared on the floor (v14).

Moses/Aaron told them that it was bad/bread (v15) and they should all gather as much as they needed.

Some gathered loads/toads and others gathered little/lots (v17), but when they measured it, everyone had the right amount!

Read verses 19-20

Moses said *"No one should keep any bread until evening/morning/Christmas"* (v19). But some of them ignored Moses. In the morning their bread was full of magic/maggots and began to see/hear/smell (v20).

Yuck!

The Israelites had already learned that they could **trust** God and should **obey** Him.

But some of them still didn't **trust** God to give them enough food. And so they refused to **obey** His commands.

Pray!

Read Exodus 20 v 1-17. Which of God's commands do you need to take more seriously and obey more? What will you do about it? Ask for God's help.

Bad mannas

God is giving the Israelites bread from heaven!

For five days, they collected the same amount of bread, but on the sixth day they had to do something different...

WEIRD WORDS

Two omers
About four litres

Holy Sabbath
The special day on which God said everyone should rest from work

Read Exodus 16 v 21-26

Complete the table to show what changed. Circle the answers.

DAY	How much manna was collected?	Was the previous day's bread fresh?
1-5	None / Usual amount / Twice as much	YES NO
6	None / Usual amount / Twice as much	YES NO
7	None / Usual amount / Twice as much	YES NO

The seventh day (the Sabbath) was a special day to rest from work. God told them not to collect bread on this special day of the week. In fact, there would be none left for them to collect!

Yesterday we saw what happened when some people collected too much bread. Maggots! Yuck!

Surely they won't disobey God again! They're not stupid enough to look for food when God has told them not to. Or are they???

Read verses 27-30

Did the Israelites follow God's instructions?

All obeyed God ☐
Some obeyed God ☐
None obeyed God ☐

*In your own words, write down what God said about the Israelites (it's in **verse 28**).*

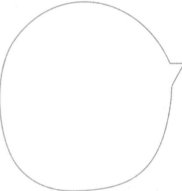

Pray!

Say sorry to God for specific times recently when you have disobeyed Him. Ask Him to help you to obey Him more and more.

Remember remember

**Exodus
16 v 31-36**

*Circle the ones
you never forget:*

Your birthday

Mum's birthday

Homework

*That God loves
you loads*

> Are you coming to
> football on Saturday?

> Thanks for reminding
> me, I'd forgotten all
> about it!

Do you ever forget stuff? Over the
last few days, we've seen how the
Israelites kept forgetting how great
God had been to them. So God told
Moses to do something to remind
them in the future.

Read Exodus 16 v 31-34

They called the bread **manna** which
means *"What is it?"*

When they first saw the bread
covering the ground, they had no
idea what it was!

*Fill in what God commanded the
people to do (v33).*

Take a j_____ and put

_____

of m_____ in it

They kept a jar of manna in a special
place, so that the Israelites could see
it for many years to come. It would
remind them that God gave them
food in the desert after He rescued
them from Egypt. It reminded them
that God was always looking after
them.

Action!

The Bible reminds us how great God
is to us. If you sometimes forget
what you've learned in the Bible,
why not write it down in a diary or
notebook to remind you? Or you
could set a reminder in your phone.

Read verses 35-36

The Israelites travelled in the desert
for 40 years! And **every day** God
gave them enough bread to eat!
God doesn't only look after us on
some days, but then forget us on
others. God gives us what we need
every day.

Pray!

Thank God that He loves you ALL
THE TIME. Thank Him that He
gives you exactly what you need.

Water and whine

**Exodus
17 v 1-7**

*God has been
so good to the
Israelites.*

*He has rescued
them from
Egypt, fed them
in the desert
and has been
so patient with
them.*

WEIRD WORDS

Livestock
Animals

Elders
Leaders

Staff
Walking stick

The Nile
River in Egypt

Massah
Means *testing*

Meribah
Means *arguing*

Yet the Israelites are still refusing to trust and obey God! Will they never learn???

Read Exodus 17 v 1-3

and fill in the spaces.

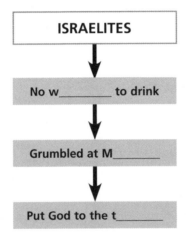

ISRAELITES

↓

No w_____ to drink

↓

Grumbled at M_____

↓

Put God to the t_____

How would Moses deal with this tricky situation?

Read verse 4

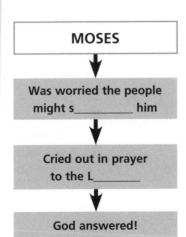

MOSES

↓

Was worried the people might s_____ him

↓

Cried out in prayer to the L_____

↓

God answered!

Read verses 5-7

The Israelites just **complained** about the lack of water. But Moses **asked God for help**. And God answered him by making water flow out of a rock!

YOU

↓

Arguing with parents?

↓

Bullied at school?

↓

COMPLAIN or ASK GOD FOR HELP?

Pray!

What do you do when things are tough? Tell God about any problems you have at the moment. Ask Him to help you.

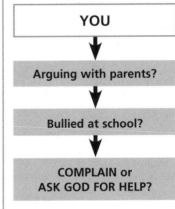

Arms v army

**Exodus
17 v 8-16**

Bread from heaven! Water from a rock!

What amazing thing will God do next for His people?

Oh look, the Israelites are in trouble again! This time they are being attacked by the evil Amalekites. What's worse is that the Israelites have never fought a battle before!

But God is with them…

Read Exodus 17 v 8-16

Spot the ten mistakes in the story below. Circle each one.

> **The Amalekites came and attacked the Israelites in Manchester. Moses said to Joshua, "Choose some children to go and dance with the Amalekites. I will stand on top of the ladder with the staff of God."**
> **As long as Moses held up his feet, the Israelites were winning. But when he lowered his hands, the Eskimos were winning. When Moses' hands grew tired, he sat on a sofa. Aaron and Miriam held his hands up high until morning. So Joshua defeated the Ethiopians.**

As long as Moses held up his h_____ the Israelites were w_____ (v11)

Moses lifted his hands up to **ask God's help.** Moses knew they couldn't win the battle on their own; they needed God. So he prayed and prayed and prayed until God gave them the victory.

In those days people often stood to pray with their hands held up. You can pray like that too if you want— but you don't have to!

You can pray sitting, standing… at home, at school, outside… **anywhere and anytime.**

Prayer Challenge!

Find three unusual places to pray today. (On a bus? Up a tree? In the bath?) Each time, thank God that you can pray anywhere, anytime. Ask Him to help you to trust Him as Moses did.

Answers: Manchester, children, dance, ladder, feet, Eskimos, sofa, Miriam, morning, Ethiopians.

Name game

**Exodus
18 v 1-8**

*God helped
Moses and the
Israelites defeat
the Amalekites.*

*Now it's time
to meet Moses'
family...*

WEIRD WORDS

**Mountain of
God**
Mount Sinai, a
special mountain
for God and the
Israelites. It's where
God would give
them the Ten
Commandments.

Hardships
Troubles and
problems

---

*Are there any people in your family
with strange and interesting names?*

There are some strange names in
Moses' family...

Read Exodus 18 v 1-4

Find the names in the wordsearch.

```
G E Z G V D N J
E L I E Z E R E
H Q P R T A J T
C H P S L Z Y H
S M O H K F B R
K D R O M F G O
Z J A M O S E S
A E H L X B C U
```

Z_____ was Moses'
wife. Her dad J_____
was M_____
father-in-law. Moses called
his sons G_____
and E_____

Moses gave his sons special names.
Gershom means *foreigner* because
the Israelites had been slaves in the
foreign land of Egypt. **Eliezer** means
God is my helper because God
had rescued the Israelites from evil
Pharaoh in Egypt.

Read verses 5-8

Moses told Jethro about all the
amazing things God had done for
the Israelites.

Action!

Who can YOU tell about all the
great things God has done for you?

_____

_____

_____

Pray!

Ask God to give you the courage
and the words to tell these people
about the great things He has
done for you.

Jethro's joy

**Exodus
18 v 9-12**

Moses has been
telling his father-
in-law, Jethro, all
about how God
had rescued the
Israelites from
Egypt.

*Read the verses to see how Jethro
reacted to what Moses told him. Fill
in the gaps using the **word pool**,
then read what we can learn from
Jethro.*

**burnt   delighted   God
gods   Egyptians   Jethro
know   Lord   greater
Israelites   Pharaoh
Praise   sacrifices**

1. Really happy!
Read Exodus 18 v 9

Jethro was d_____

to hear about what

G_____ had done for the

I_____

When you read about God, does it
make you happy? Are you excited to
hear what God has done for you?

For Christians, the great news that
Jesus rescued them from sin is really
exciting!

2. Praise God!
Read verse 10

Jethro said "P_____ the

L_____ who rescued you

from P_____ and

the E_____"

What can YOU praise God for?

_____

_____

3. God is best!
Read verse 11

Jethro said "Now I k_____

that the Lord is g_____

than all other g_____"

Jethro realised that God is the ONLY
true God. Do you believe that God
is the only true God? Is He first in
your life, or are other things more
important to you?

4. Giving to God
Read verse 12

J_____ brought a

b_____ offering and

other s_____

to God.

Jethro gave these sacrifices to God
to show that he was serious about
living God's way. Jesus sacrificed
Himself so we can live God's way by
following Him. How serious are you
about that?

Pray!

Read through those four things
again. Is there something you
need to talk to God about or ask
His help with?

78

**Exodus
18 v 13-27**

*Jethro is visiting
his son-in-law
Moses.*

WEIRD WORDS

Seek God's will
Find out what God
wants them to do

Dispute
Disagreement

Decrees
Commands

**People's
representative**
Moses told the
people what God
wanted to say to
them

Fear God
Giving God the
respect and
obedience He
deserves

Dishonest gain
Stealing

Advice squad

Read Exodus 18 v 13-23

*Then answer these YES/NO
questions.*

**Did Moses help people to
make wise decisions that
pleased God (v16)?**
YES/NO _____

**Was Jethro happy with
Moses doing all this
work (v17)?**
YES/NO _____

**Was it too much work for
Moses to do alone?**
YES/NO _____

**Did Moses needs lots of
helpers (v18)?**
YES/NO _____

**Did it matter whether
the helpers loved and
served God (v21)?**
YES/NO _____

Jethro knew that Moses was trying
to do too much by himself. Moses
could serve God even better if he
had lots of help! Christian workers
often have soooo much to do. They
need help from other Christians!

Action!

Who has too much to do at your
church?

_____

How can YOU help them out?

_____

_____

_____

Phone or email them to offer your
help! Go on!

Read verses 24-27

**Did Moses take Jethro's
advice (v24)?**
Yes/No _____

Older Christians often have wise
and helpful advice for us. Listen to
them! (And if you're not sure about
their advice, check it with what the
Bible says.)

Think!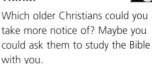

Which older Christians could you
take more notice of? Maybe you
could ask them to study the Bible
with you.

Pray!

Ask God to give you an
opportunity to help out Christians
who are overloaded with work.

John: The real Jesus

**John
11 v 1-6**

*Today we're
going back into
John's Gospel,
to discover more
about who Jesus
really is.*

WEIRD WORDS

**Mary and
Martha**
For more about
them, check out
Luke 10 v 38-42 and
John 12 v 1-8

For God's glory
So that God will
get the praise and
honour He deserves

Read John 11 v 1-3

Mary and Martha's brother is really
ill. So what do the sisters do? Cross
out the Ks, Xs and Zs to find out.

**KTHZEZYSKENZXDAMZK
ESSXAGEKXTOJXESZUSK**

_____

_____

_____

Think!

When something goes wrong in
your life (maybe someone you know
is ill), do you tell Jesus about it? Do
you ask for His help? Maybe there's
something you want to talk to Him
about right now?

Read verse 4

Even though Lazarus will probably
die, Jesus knows this story won't
end in death.

*What does Jesus say is the reason
for Lazarus' illness?*

**ZITIKKSFXZXORXGK
OZZDSXGLKXORZYKZ**

_____

_____

In the end, everyone will see how
awesome God is!

**KANZZDGXKOZDSXSONZK
WIZZLLBKEGLOXXRIZKX
FIZZEDTXHRKOUXGHZIT**

_____

_____

People will also see how awesome
Jesus (God's Son) is!

So it looks as if Jesus will heal
Lazarus straightaway. Right?

Er... read verses 5-6

Lazarus is seriously ill. But instead of
rushing off to heal him, Jesus hung
around for two days!!! Here's why...

**Jesus was going to raise Lazarus
from death. If He waited several
days (until the body stank!), no
one could claim that Lazarus
hadn't really been dead!**

Pray!

Thank God that His timing is
always perfect, even when it
seems strange to us.

**John
11 v 7-16**

Lazarus was really sick.

His sisters Mary and Martha had sent for Jesus.

But Jesus hung around for two whole days before setting off to where Lazarus lived.

Sick sense

Read John 11 v 7-8, 16

What were the disciples worried about? Put it into your own words.

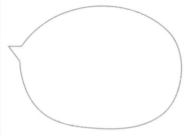

Thomas was convinced that they would all be killed by the Jewish leaders (v16)! But at least he had the courage to go with Jesus.

Read verses 9-10

What did Jesus say?

That's a bit baffling. Jesus was saying that it wasn't yet time for Him to die. The Jews wouldn't decide when He died. **It was God's decision!** The Jewish leaders were stumbling in the dark, but Jesus knew what He was doing. **It was all part of God's perfect plan!**

Read verses 11-15

Because Jesus wasn't there to save Lazarus, he died.

But Jesus was going to raise Lazarus back to life.

Why did Jesus do it this way (v15)?

Wow!

Jesus wanted His disciples to believe that He was God's Son. To believe that He had power over death. And to realise that He would save people from their sins. And He wants you to believe it too! Do you?

Deadly serious

**John
11 v 17-27**

Rapid recap!

Jesus' friend Lazarus was really ill.

But Jesus wouldn't rush to help him.

Lazarus died before Jesus arrived.

WEIRD WORDS

Resurrection
When God's people will be raised back to life, to live with Him for ever

The Messiah
The King who would rescue God's people

Amazingly, Lazarus' sister Martha hadn't given up hope.

Read John 11 v 17-22

Martha had wanted Jesus to heal Lazarus before he died. Yet what did she say (v22)? Go back one letter to find out.

__ __ __ __   __ __ __
F W F O   O P X

__ __ __   __ __ __ __
H P E   X J M M

__ __ __ __   __ __ __
H J W F   Z P V

__ __ __ __ __ __ __ __
X I B U F W F S

__ __ __   __ __ __
Z P V   B T L

Martha believed Jesus could bring Lazarus back to life!

Read verses 23-24

Martha believed that Lazarus would come back to life on the day of God's judgment. But Jesus told her something she didn't know...

Read verses 25-26. Twice.

What does Jesus mean?

*Fill in the gaps with the words **life**, **death**, **die** and **live**.*

Jesus is the resurrection and the _____. Whoever turns to Him will _____ with Him for ever! Even though their bodies will physically _____, Jesus rescues them from _____ in hell. They will _____ with Jesus for ever!

This is so important! If you don't understand it, ask a Christian friend what v25-26 mean.

> For a free e-booklet called *Why did Jesus rise?* email discover@thegoodbook.co.uk or check out www.thegoodbook.co.uk/contact-us to find our UK mailing address.

Read verse 27

Think & pray!

Can you truthfully say what Martha says in v27? If so, why not tell Jesus right now?

John
11 v 28-37

Mary and Martha's brother is dead.

Yesterday we saw how Martha believed that Jesus could bring Lazarus back to life.

But what about Mary?

Crying out loud

Read John 11 v 28-31

When Mary heard that Jesus was there, she rushed out to meet Him.

Think!

Are you excited about Jesus? Do you long to spend time with Him?

Read verses 32-35

Mary was so upset by Lazarus' death. How did Jesus react? Fill in the vowels (aeiou) to find out.

1. J__sus w__s __pset __nd tr__ __bl__d (v33)

2. J__s__s w__pt (v35)

Wow!

Jesus cares deeply about His friends. When we're upset, He's there to comfort us. We can turn to Him. If you're upset about something, why not tell Jesus about it right now? Ask Him to help you.

Jesus is a great example to us. He showed sympathy to Mary. And we should show support and sympathy to people when they are down.

Action!

Who do you know who is hurting right now?

_____

_____

How can you show support and sympathy to them?

_____

_____

_____

_____

Will you talk to them and pray for them? Ask God to help you say the right things.

Read verses 36-37

Some people thought Jesus was a fake. They wouldn't believe that He was God's Son. They wouldn't believe that He could raise Lazarus back to life. Tomorrow, we'll see if Jesus could…

Life saver

Flick back to **John 11 v 22** and **27** to see what Martha had said to Jesus.

> **God will give you whatever you ask. I believe you are God's Son.**

Now she's having her doubts.

Some people couldn't understand why Jesus didn't heal Lazarus before he died.

But now they're going to see something far more spectacular!

Read John 11 v 38-39

> **Lazarus has been dead for four days. His body will stink!**

We all have our doubts sometimes. But now Jesus is going to reveal the truth...

Read verses 40-44

Jesus raised Lazarus back to life! He has power over death! *But why did He do this amazing miracle? Find two reasons.*

Take every second letter, starting with the first S. Then start again with the second S for the second reason.

WEIRD WORDS

Odour
Smell

Glory of God
God's greatness

Linen
Cloth

1. S_____

_____

_____ (v40)

Jesus wants everyone to see how awesome and powerful God is.

2. S_____

_____

_____ (v42)

Jesus wants people to believe that God sent Him to earth to rescue us from our sins!

Think & pray!

You've read all about Jesus. Maybe you've seen His effect on people's lives. But do you believe that He is God's Son? That He was sent to rescue you from your sinful ways?
Have you turned to Him?
Had your sins forgiven?
Do you live your life for Him?
Talk to God about your answer.

S S O O T T H H
D T S H E A E T G A Y
E L N O T R Y Y
L E F G O B
V S S U S M O
E U D U O
O E U L W I O

Wicked plot/Great plan

**John
11 v 45-53**

*Jesus has raised
Lazarus back to
life to show that
He is God's Son.*

*Let's check out
the crowd's
reaction to
this incredible
miracle.*

WEIRD WORDS

Sanhedrin
Council of the most
important Jewish
leaders

Signs
Miracles

Perish
Be destroyed

Prophesied
Predicted

Read John 11 v 45-46

Some people believed that Jesus
was God's Son. Others didn't. Even
today, people are still split over who
Jesus really is.

Read verses 47-48

The Jewish leaders were worried
that Jesus would become so popular
that they would lose their power
over the people. Then the Romans
would destroy the Jewish nation.

Read verses 49-50

What did Caiaphas say?

*Start in the shaded square and
follow the maze.*

I		D	E	D	E	T	A	N
T	I	O	Y	E	B	I	L	E
B	S	R	T	S	N	O	O	H
E	F	O	R	O	I	E	T	W
T	R	M	E	N	D	A	H	E
T	E	A	N	T	O	N	T	H

— —

— — — — — —

— — — — — — —

— — — — —

— — — — — — — —

— — — — — — — —

What Caiaphas said has a double
meaning!

**Caiaphas meant that they
should kill Jesus to save the
Jews from being destroyed
by the Romans.**

**Jesus' death would save
people. But not from the
Romans! It would save
people from the punishment
they deserve for their sins!**

And not just Jewish people...

Read verses 51-53

Wow!

God would use this WICKED PLOT
to carry out His WONDERFUL PLAN
to rescue people from their sinful
ways!

Pray!

Do you want to thank God for
His amazing plan to rescue people
from their sins?

John
11 v 54-57

The chief priests and Pharisees are out to kill Jesus.

Maybe they'll grab Him before the Passover feast in Jerusalem...

Feast your eyes on this

Read John 11 v 54-57

Jesus was going to die, to rescue His people. But not yet. The Pharisees wouldn't decide when Jesus died. God was in control, not them!

> **So what's this Passover festival all about?**

Passover Fact File

Passover was held to remember God rescuing the Israelites from Egypt (over 1000 years earlier).

God had sent 10 plagues on Egypt, but Pharaoh wouldn't let the Israelites go.

Pharaoh only let them go after God killed the eldest sons of all the Egyptians.

The Israelites had to do something special so that their sons were not killed too.

Here's what they had to do...

1. K__ll a l__ __b
Read Exodus 12 v 3-6

The lamb was killed instead of the firstborn (eldest) son in each Israelite family. The eldest son could say: *"That lamb died instead of me!"*

Wow!

The lamb's death is a picture of what Jesus would do. He died on the cross to take the punishment we should get for our sins. So Christians can say: *"He died instead of me!"*

2. Use the lamb's bl__ __d
Read Exodus 12 v 7, 12-13

They had to put the lamb's blood on their door frames. No blood would have meant death for the eldest son.

But if there was blood there, God promised to

p__ __s o__ __ __ (v13)

the house and not kill the eldest son in that house.

Think!

Have you trusted Jesus to save you from the punishment you deserve? If so, then one day God will come to judge everyone, but He will PASS OVER you because Jesus died instead of you!

86

John
12 v 1-11

On His way to
the Passover
feast in
Jerusalem, Jesus
stopped off at
the village of
Bethany.

He visited
Mary, Martha
and Lazarus
—remember
them?

WEIRD WORDS

Passover
See yesterday's
Discover

Faith
Belief, trust

Mary's hairy story

Read John 12 v 1-3

Mary was so grateful for all that
Jesus had done for her. Including
bringing her brother Lazarus back to
life! She just had to show her love.

*Spot two unusual things (in v3)
about what Mary did for Jesus.*

1. The per_____ was
very ex_____

It was worth a year's pay! It would
cost thousands these days. That's
how much she loved Jesus!

Action!

Do you make costly sacrifices for
Jesus? Like giving time to Him
instead of pleasing yourself? What
will you do for Jesus?

_____

_____

_____

_____

2. Mary wiped Jesus'
f_____ with her h_____

Only slaves would normally go near
dusty, stinky feet. And not with their
hair! Mary was very humble, putting
Jesus first.

But not everyone was pleased.

Read verses 4-6
Who wasn't pleased?

J_____   I_____

Read verses 7-8
Who was pleased?

J_____

Who's the one that really counts?

J_____

Jesus knew this was a rare chance to
serve Him before He died.

Wow!

Sometimes people will criticise
your efforts to serve Jesus. But He
is pleased — and that's what's
important.

Pray!

Ask God to help you to do the
things for Jesus that you wrote
down earlier.

Read verses 9-11. Notice that the chief priests are still up to no good!

87 Return of the King

John 12 v 12-19

The Jewish leaders want to kill Jesus.

So will He sneak quietly into Jerusalem?

No chance!

WEIRD WORDS

Hosanna!
Save us!

Blessed
Given great things by God

Daughter Zion
Jerusalem

Colt
Young male donkey

Glorified
Raised back to life

Read John 12 v 12-13

The people went crazy for Jesus! What did they call Him?

They thought Jesus was the King who God had promised would rescue them.

They were right!

They thought He was a mighty warrior who would bash the Romans.

They were wrong!

Read verses 14-15

Instead of a warhorse, Jesus rode on a donkey! Just as the prophet Zechariah had said 500 years earlier!

Look up Zechariah 9 v 9-11

What did he say Jesus the King would do?

---

1. _ _ _ _ _

2. _ _ _ _   _ _ _ _

3. _ _ _ _ _

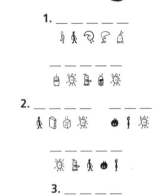

Wow!

But Jesus wouldn't do these things by fighting the Romans. He would die on the cross to free people who are prisoners to sin. And He will rule as their King in heaven!

Read John 12 v 16-19

Jesus' followers only realised what amazing things He had done after He died and rose again.

Pray!

If Jesus has freed you from sin, then spend some time praising and thanking Him!

A	B	C	E	F	G	H	I	K	L	N	O	P	R	S	T	U

John
12 v 20-26

Get your brain in gear, because today we've got four top truths to learn from Jesus.

(Fill in the vowels for the answers.)

WEIRD WORDS

The Festival
Passover

Philip
One of the twelve disciples

Be glorified
Die and be raised back to life

Eternal
Everlasting

Seed of truth

TOP TRUTH 1:

J_S_S C_M_ F_R
TH_ WH_L_ W_RLD

Read John 12 v 20-22

These Greek people show us that Jesus didn't just come for Jewish people, but Gentiles (non-Jews) too. **Anyone can turn to Jesus to have their wrongs forgiven!**

TOP TRUTH 2:

J_S_S' D_ _TH
G_V_S L_F_!

Read verses 23-24

A seed must fall from a plant and die before a new plant can grow from it. Jesus knew that He would soon **die** (v23). But His death will bring eternal life to anyone who turns to Him for forgiveness.

TOP TRUTH 3:

WE MUST L_V_
G_D, NOT L_F_

Read verse 25

People who live to enjoy life instead of living to please God will be punished. But people who put God first will live with Him for ever!

TOP TRUTH 4:

WE MUST S_RV_ J_S_S

Read verse 26

If you're serious about following Jesus, then you've got to show it in the way you live your life. And then God will honour you!

Action!

What can you change in your life to serve Jesus more?

_____

_____

_____

_____

_____

_____

Ask God to help you.

**John
12 v 27-33**

George has got a science test tomorrow.

He hates science and knows he'll fail.

He wishes it would just go away.

Cross examination

Jesus was dreading something too. But He was facing something much worse: His death.

Read John 12 v 27-30

Jesus thought about asking His Father to save Him from death on the cross. Instead, what did Jesus say? Go back one letter to find out.

__ __   __ __ __
J U   X B T

__ __ __   __ __ __ __
G P S   U I J T

__ __ __ __ __ __   __
S F B T P O   J

__ __ __ __   __ __
D B N F   U P

__ __ __ __   __ __ __ __
U I J T   I P V S

The **whole purpose** of Jesus coming to earth was to die on the cross and take God's punishment in our place! This amazing event brought glory to God (v28).

Read verses 31-33

Find four awesome things that Jesus' death would do.

1. __ __ __ __ __ __ __
   H M P S J G Z

   __ __ __ (v28)
   H P E

People would see how amazing God is!

2. __ __ __ __ __   __ __ __
   K V E H F   U I F

   __ __ __ __ __ (v31)
   X P S M E

People who turn to God will be rescued from sin. Those who don't will be punished.

3. __ __ __ __ __   __ __ __
   E S J W F   P V U

   __ __ __   __ __ __ __ __
   U I F   E F W J M

Jesus' death and resurrection would defeat the devil once and for all! (v31)

4. __ __ __ __   __ __ __
   E S B X   B M M

   __ __ __ __ __ __   __ __
   Q F P Q M F   U P

   __ __ __ __ __ __ __ (v32)
   I J N T F M G

Jesus' death would make it possible for anyone to live with Him for ever

Pray!

Read through those four things again, praising God for what Jesus' death has done for you.

Light and wrong

**John
12 v 34-41**

Jesus has just told the people that He is going to die and that He will judge the world, beat the devil and rescue people from sin!

But they just don't seem to get it.

Read John 12 v 34-36

and fill in the missing first letters of some of the words.

The __rowd didn't __nderstand what __esus had been __alking about.

Jesus called Himself the __ight. He __old them to __ut their __rust in the __ight so that they didn't end up in __arkness.

Wow!

In other words, Jesus is saying: *"Follow me, trust in me, live for me! Don't live the dark, ungodly way that everyone else does!"*

Think!

What area of your life do you need to sort out, so that you're living in light, and not in darkness?

_____

_____

_____

_____

So did they listen to Jesus and believe Him?

Read verses 37-41

Despite all the __iracles they had seen, they still would __ot __elieve in __esus! (v37)
The __rophet __saiah had said this would __appen (v38). Isaiah said that __ecause __eople __ejected __od, God __linded __heir __yes (v40).

When people refuse to turn to God, they cannot see what a terrible mistake they're making.

Pray!

Ask God to help you to live His way. And to turn your back on the dark, ungodly way you used to live.

This is your last chance to listen in on Jesus this issue!

Ask God to help you understand what He wants to say to you.

Listen up!

Read John 12 v 42-43

Some important people believed in Jesus. But they were too scared to admit it. What was the problem? Fill in the vowels.

**Th__y l__v__d
pr__ __s__ fr__m
p__ __pl__ m__r__ th__n
pr__ __s__ fr__m
G__d (v43).**

Think!

Do you stand up for your belief in Jesus? Or are you more bothered about what people think of you?

Read verses 44-46

**If someone sees me,
th__y s__ __
th__ __n__ wh__
s__nt m__ (v45).**

Jesus is God! Got that?

**No one wh__
b__l__ __v__s __n
m__ sh__ __ld st__y
__n d__rkn__ss (v46).**

What are you doing to get away from your old sinful ways? (Look back to yesterday's *Think!* section.)

Read verses 47-48

**Th__r__ is a
j__dg__ f__r th__ __n__
wh__ r__j__cts m__ (v48).**

Jesus came to **save** people, not judge them. But anyone who rejects Jesus will be judged and punished.

Read verses 49-50

Why should we listen to Jesus?

**Wh__t__v__r I s__y __s
wh__t th__ F__th__r h__s
t__ld m__ t__ s__y.
H__s c__mm__nd
l__ __ds t__
__t__rn__l l__f__ (v50).**

Jesus speaks the words of God the Father. If we obey them, we will trust in Jesus and have eternal life with Him!

Pray!

Read today's verses again, asking God to help you fully understand them.

DISCOVER
COLLECTION

DISCOVER ISSUE 7

Join the Israelites in an epic construction project in Exodus. Discover more about Jesus' unbeatable love in John. James gives us great advice for living God's way. And get a glorious glimpse of the future in Revelation.

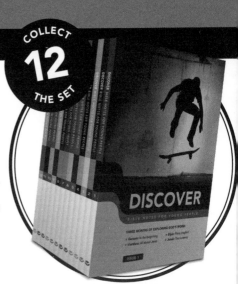

ISSUE 7

COLLECT 12 THE SET

COLLECT ALL 12 ISSUES TO COMPLETE THE DISCOVER COLLECTION

Don't forget to order the next issue of Discover. Or even better, grab a one-year subscription to make sure Discover lands in your hands as soon as it's out. Packed full of puzzles, prayers and pondering points.

thegoodbook.co.uk thegoodbook.com

thegoodbook
COMPANY